Jesus —
Name Above All
Names

Jesus —
Name Above All Names

Kenneth Hagin Jr.

Unless otherwise indicated, all Scripture quotations in this volume are from the *King James Version* of the Bible.

First Printing 1998

ISBN 0-89276-737-5

In the U.S. write:
Kenneth Hagin Ministries
P.O. Box 50126
Tulsa, OK 74150-0126

In Canada write:
Kenneth Hagin Ministries
P.O. Box 335, Station D,
Etobicoke (Toronto), Ontario
Canada, M9A 4X3

Contents

Chapter 1
There's Power in the Name!

There is saving, healing, delivering, life-giving, and life-changing power in the precious Name of Jesus! There is more power in the Name of Jesus than most of us really understand. Many Christians today talk and get excited about the Name of Jesus. But do they really understand the power in that Name?

As we begin this study on the magnificent Name of Jesus, I want to impress upon you the awesome authority that is in Jesus' Name. There's *power* in that Name!

Years ago, a certain corporation initiated a clever ad campaign using the slogan, "When _____ speaks, *everybody* listens." Television commercials would feature crowds of people busily going about their everyday affairs. But as soon as the company name was mentioned, everyone suddenly stopped "dead still"!

That catchy slogan caught on and was very effective. It was so effective, in fact, that thousands began to recognize this company by its slogan, and the rest is history.

1

Well, I want to let you know that at the matchless Name of Jesus, everything stops — comes to a standstill — in Heaven, on the earth, and under the earth! In other words, everything halts and comes to attention at the sound of that precious Name! Why? Because the Scripture says, *"That at the name of Jesus every knee should bow, of things in heaven, and things in earth, and things under the earth"* (Phil. 2:10).

Authority in Heaven

When you speak the Name of Jesus, everything in Heaven stands still. I can imagine the heavenly angels standing at attention, saying, "They're speaking that Name on earth. Do we need to prepare for an earthly mission? Yes, someone needs deliverance, and he's speaking that Name!"

You see, that Name is known throughout the regions of those heavenly golden streets. And when the sound of that Name — Jesus — ascends on High, every heavenly body stands at attention.

From reading the Scriptures, it sounds as if the Heavenly Father Himself stops everything He's doing at the mention of the Name of His Son Jesus. Jesus said, "Ask the Father *in My Name*, and He will give you whatever you ask" (John 16:23).

The Name of Jesus is powerful! And we need to thoroughly understand that fact if we are to benefit from the mighty power of the Name.

PHILIPPIANS 2:10
10 That at the name of Jesus every knee should bow, of things IN HEAVEN, and things IN EARTH, and things UNDER THE EARTH.

We talked briefly about the Name of Jesus in Heaven. Now let's talk about the Name of Jesus on the earth.

Did you know that every problem or anything that comes against you — demons, disease, poverty, and the circumstances of life — must come under subjection to the Name of Jesus when that Name is spoken with authority? All of these problems must come to a halt! If those problems could talk, they'd say, *"Oh, no, we hope they're not coming after us with that Name!"*

There's also power *under the earth* in the Name of Jesus. Every being under the earth — every angel who was kicked out of Heaven for disobedience and became a fallen angel or evil spirit — knows and understands the power of the Name of Jesus! They tremble at the sound of that Name (James 2:19)!

I remember hearing the story of a young Christian musician who'd been invited to some type of concert featuring several secular artists and bands.

At the concert, this Christian musician was introduced, but the crowd of thousands was so busy partying that no one seemed to pay any attention to him when he came on stage.

So the young man just went over to the piano, sat down, and began to skillfully run his fingers over the keys. At the same time, he spoke into the microphone, *"Jesus."* By the time the musician repeated that Name about four or five times, the entire place had become as quiet and still as a graveyard.

The power of the evil one was present in that crowd. But at the Name of Jesus, every demon had to stop in its tracks!

All that musician had to do was say, "Jesus." He didn't pray; he just used the Name. When he got the crowd's attention, he sang a couple of Christian songs. Then he said, "I'll be behind the stage if anyone wants to know more about this Jesus I've been singing about." Many young people, perhaps even hundreds, met him backstage to hear what he had to say!

That's what the Name of Jesus can do!

The Power of the Name
In the Situations of Life

Just the mention of the Name of Jesus can bring peace and rest in the midst of the storm. Sometimes just repeating that Name two or three times brings a tangible anointing on the scene.

I have used that Name many, many times, but I particularly remember using it as I've traveled overseas. Now I'm not talking about using the Name of Jesus just in a church service or meeting. I'm talking about dealing with a potentially dangerous situation, such as a demon-possessed person who is walking down the same street you are! That has happened to me. What did I do? I just began to quietly say, "In the Name of Jesus. In the Name of Jesus" until I was safely past all the commotion.

"Well, why didn't you cast the devil out of that person?" someone may ask. First, because no one asked me to, and the Lord didn't lead me to. And second, I don't have any authority in the Name of Jesus over others without their permission. But I do have authority where my own life is concerned.

Also, sometimes in dealing with customs, I've had to use my authority in the Name of Jesus. I once stood in a customs line where there was chaos all around me. The customs officers were screaming at one another. The situation kept getting worse, and I could see the unrest among those standing in the line.

So I just began to speak the Name! I said it about five or six times: "In the Name of Jesus . . . ."

Suddenly, everything quieted down, and the customs officials just started waving a bunch of us through without even checking our luggage. After I left and rounded the corner, all of a sudden, someone started hollering, and the commotion started up again. You see, there's power in the Name of Jesus! When you are in the presence of danger, you have a right to control the "atmosphere" with the Name!

Incident in Taipei, Taiwan

The awesome power of the Name of Jesus delivered me from certain death when I was stationed overseas in Taipei, Taiwan. You may have heard me tell about the time I was riding my motorcycle with a group of friends over mountainous terrain just outside of Taipei. Riding back into town that night, I nearly had a fatal accident.

The wind was blowing vigorously, and we were riding pretty fast. I was at the tail-end of our caravan of motorcycles. As I came around a bend in the road, a gust of wind picked my bike up! I knew there was at least a thousand-foot drop off that narrow road. When my bike hit the ground, it was sliding toward the edge of the cliff, and one wheel did slide over the edge. There was nothing under the wheel of that bike but a thousand feet of air!

And if it weren't for the Name of Jesus, I would have gone crashing down in the canyon below!

When my bike skidded toward that canyon, there was really nothing I could do. I was "kicking gears" and clenching my teeth. All I had time to say was, "Jesus!"

When I yelled out that Name, it was as if someone suddenly picked up my bike and set it back down on the pavement. I'd had the brakes on, so once both wheels were back on the road, my bike made a tire mark as I skidded across the road and partway up the side of a mountain on the opposite side of the street. Then I came back down onto the road before coming to a screeching stop.

Afterward, some of the guys I was with went back to the site with flashlights, and we could see where my tire had made a mark as it went off the side of the road. Then we could see another mark where the tire was "placed" back on the road and where it went up the side of the mountain across the street.

Some of the guys said, "Man, you were lucky." I said, "No, I wasn't lucky. Luck had nothing to do with it. The hand of God reached down and gave my motorcycle a little 'push'!"

Why? Because of the Name! Because I uttered the Name of Jesus.

Notice I was in danger at that terrifying moment, and I didn't have time to pray about it. I didn't have time to fast or pray! I was caught in an "impossible" situation in the dark mountains of Taipei, and the devil was there, too, trying to steal, kill, and destroy. All I had time to do was yell out the Name of Jesus.

Many Christians don't fully realize the protecting power that is in the Name of Jesus. But that same power is available to us today.

If Christians understood the power that's in the Name of Jesus, they wouldn't be fasting and praying and going through a lot of rigmarole, trying to get victory. Thank God for fasting and praying. I don't want to minimize them in the least, because they have their place. But there's *power* in the Name! We need to understand, focus on, and have faith in the power that's in the Name. Instead, many are putting their faith in much praying and long fasts.

Actually, you should never go on a long fast unless you know for *certain* that God told you to do it. If God told you to do it, He'll take care of your physical body. But if God *didn't* tell you to do it, you could seriously harm your body.

I went on a particularly long fast once, but I knew God was dealing with me to do it. My wife knew it was God, too, because she knows that in the natural, I can't fast for very many days! It just doesn't work well for me.

When I went on that fast, I drank a glass of juice every day and plenty of water (you have to keep fluids in your body, or you'll dehydrate). And I didn't go around "broadcasting" that I was fasting. You can lose everything you're fasting and praying for if you broadcast to others what you're doing. Fasting and praying should be between you and God.

But there's power in the Name of Jesus! There is victory in His Name! I have seen that power demonstrated in the lives of others, and I've experienced it many times in my own life.

'Pat's Momma'

When I was just a young boy, I had another unusual experience that illustrates the power in that Name.

When I was a kid, I often stayed overnight at my grandmother's. She was my dad's mom, and all the grandchildren called her "Pat's Momma." She got her name, because one of her young grandchildren would always refer to her as Pat's Momma (Pat was my dad's youngest brother, who was still living at home at the time). Pretty soon, all the grandchildren started calling her Pat's Momma, and even townspeople and friends began calling her by that name!

Pat's Momma had become blind while carrying her youngest child, Pat. Her blindness was somehow caused by a series of emotional events that happened in her life. My dad's father, her husband, left her when my dad was very young. They had four children, and it was a very traumatic time in her life. Back then, they didn't know as much as they do now, and some doctor who was trying to help her did something that caused her to be blind permanently.

Pat's Momma told me when I was older, "Son, you are the only one of the grandkids that I've ever seen; I saw you in a vision as I was praying." (This was after I had made my decision to answer the call of God and become a minister. She told me that in the vision, she saw me preaching to large crowds of many different nationalities. Well, thank God, I've been able to do that!)

Her father, my great-grandfather, "Grandpa Drake," had quite a bit of money when the Depression hit. Everyone thought that he retained a lot of his wealth, and the rumor spread throughout the town that he had given my grandmother, his only daughter, money that she kept hidden in a trunk in her closet.

Well, there really wasn't anything in that trunk but quilts! But it seems people were often trying to break into Pat's Momma's house! I remember when I was about six years old, I was at Pat's Momma's house when someone tried to break in.

I was already in bed and asleep on this particular night when my grandmother gently nudged me to wake me up. When I opened my eyes, she whispered, "Be quiet; don't move." So I lay there as quiet and still as I could. She whispered again, "Somebody's trying to break in." I looked and, sure enough, there was a man standing right there at the window!

The window was open, but the screen was on. I whispered to Pat's Momma, "Yes, you're right. Someone is there." She said, "Don't worry about it." Then in a whisper, she started saying, "Jesus. Jesus. Jesus."

She kept saying Jesus' Name over and over again. I watched as the man took the screen off the window. When the window was wide open, I could see the man plainly with my own eyes! I recognized him as someone who lived down the street from Pat's Momma. The man raised one leg to step through the window, but then he suddenly stopped, backed up, and tried again. He tried several times but couldn't get inside the window, so he turned around and walked away!

I hadn't said a word to Pat's Momma about recognizing the man, but the next morning she said to me, "It was So-and-so, wasn't it?" I said, "Yes. He lives right down the street."

"Don't tell your Uncle Dub," she added.

I answered, "I *can't* tell Uncle Dub; we don't even know where he is!"

Then Pat's Momma said, "While I whispered *Jesus* over and over again last night, the Lord showed me that Dub would be here in two days at four o'clock in the afternoon."

My Uncle Dub was my dad's oldest brother. He's gone home to be with the Lord now. Because of the home being broken, Dub went out on his own when he was nine years old, and before he was born again, he was meaner than a snake! For instance, one time I was walking down the street with Uncle Dub when someone spat, and some of the spittle splashed on his boot. Uncle Dub turned around and knocked the guy "into the middle of next week"! I personally witnessed it!

Uncle Dub was six feet, five inches tall. He had a 32-inch waist and wore a size 54 coat. He really stood out in a crowd. I distinctly remember seeing him, even though I was only six years old, the day he walked down that street toward Pat's Momma's house at four o'clock in the afternoon.

Dub was in the U.S. Army at the time and was the boxing champion of all three branches of the military! He'd beaten Navy boxers, Marine boxers, and Army Air Corp boxers (there was no Air Force then).

That's why my grandmother had said, "Don't you tell Uncle Dub." But being only six years old, of course, that's the first thing I did! I hollered out, "Uncle Dub, So-and-so tried to break into the house!"

"Did you see him, Son?" Uncle Dub asked.

"Yes, I saw him. He tried to get in the house. He was going to hurt us."

Right after I said that, Uncle Dub laid down his suitcase and walked out the door. I followed him out of the house and down the street. The man who'd tried to break in had a picket fence around his house. But Dub didn't even bother opening the gate. He kicked it down and walked up to the screen door, jerking it off its hinges. Then he grabbed the man, brought him out in his own front yard, and beat the fire out of him!

Someone asked, "Why didn't somebody call the police?" Someone did call, but when the policeman heard the story, he said, "Well, the man deserved it, anyway. Besides, none of us wants to go down to Pat's Momma's and mess with Dub Hagin!"

(That happened down in east Texas in a different era than we live in today. I certainly don't advocate violence as a means of settling disputes with neighbors! I just shared that with you so you'd know a little bit about what Uncle Dub was like before he got saved and sanctified!)

You see, Pat's Momma was blind and lived alone, but she had confidence in the Name of Jesus. That's why the man couldn't get in her window, no matter how hard he tried — because there's power in the Name!

Smith Wigglesworth and A Man Named Lazarus

Smith Wigglesworth used the power of the Name of Jesus in his ministry. I read his account of a church leader in Wales named Lazarus who worked in the mines during the day and preached at night. This man Lazarus followed his routine for so long that he finally broke down physically and collapsed. He contracted tuberculosis and lay bedfast and helpless for about six years.

God spoke to Wigglesworth and told him to go to Wales and raise Lazarus up. Wigglesworth went to the house where Lazarus lay on his deathbed. The man looked like a skeleton with a little skin stretched over the bones.

Wigglesworth endeavored to get him to release his faith, but Lazarus had become bitter. Others had prayed for him, and he didn't receive his healing. So Lazarus was blaming God because he hadn't received. He was bitter because he had given his whole life to God yet was in a mess physically.

Wigglesworth got seven other people. They all went into the room and gathered around Lazarus' bed, joining hands. Wigglesworth instructed them, "We are not going to pray. We are just going to use the Name of Jesus." Then they all knelt down and whispered one word: *Jesus*.

As Wigglesworth and the seven said the Name "Jesus," the power of God came down about five different times and then left. But the sixth time, it stayed on Lazarus, and Wigglesworth told him, "The power of God is on you; it's yours to accept or reject." The man's lips began to quiver, as he confessed, "I've been bitter in my heart. I know what I've done wrong. I've grieved God, and I've grieved the Spirit. Now I'm lying here helpless."

Wigglesworth said, "Repent, and God will hear you." So the man repented and said, "Oh, God, let this be to Thy glory."

Wigglesworth relates that those around the bed continued to say, "Jesus, Jesus, Jesus," causing the bed to shake. The man also began to shake. Then he got up, healed! No one laid hands on the man or prayed for him. Those gathered around his bed simply used the Name of Jesus!

I've heard many other accounts of people in the time of crisis who were delivered by using the Name. Many had been in serious accidents or deadly storms. They only had time to holler out, "Jesus! Jesus! Jesus!" And when they did, everything became calm around them, and they were kept safe!

Many of us don't fully realize the protecting power that is in the Name of Jesus, but that same power is available to us today.

The Power of the Name Against Unseen Forces

The Name of Jesus can be used against the unseen forces that surround us. Now you don't feel the oppression of the enemy in the very atmosphere as much in this country as you do when you travel outside the United States to some other countries. For example, when I was stationed in the U.S. Army for one year in Taipei, Taiwan, when I stepped off the airplane in October 1963, I actually *felt* demon oppression. I could feel it because of the Spirit of God on the inside of me. I was sensitive to the spiritual atmosphere around me.

I don't mean this disparagingly against any country of the world, but there are some countries where demon powers have more control than the power of God has control. The reason why that is so is because the majority of people who live there are under the control of demons. Maybe only a small percentage are yielded to the Spirit of God.

As I said, when I stepped off the plane in Taipei, I felt that oppression come against me, and I could hear the inward voice of the Holy Spirit saying, "Demon power." What was the Holy Spirit telling me? He was telling me to take the Name of Jesus and break any influence of demon activity against my own life. You see, you can be right in the middle of demon oppression, but if you use the Name of Jesus, it is as if you are wrapped in a "cocoon" of protection. What is that? It's the saving, healing, life-giving, life-changing, protective power of God!

Now I didn't have any authority over what was going on in that city. But I did have authority over my own life. We talked earlier about the boundaries or limits to your spiritual authority.

You have authority over your own life, and that includes the physical area where you are present at a given time. It may be a temporary dwelling, but whether the property belongs to you or not, you have a right to use the Name of Jesus for yourself — where you're concerned.

Oklahoma is a part of "Tornado Alley," where tornadoes form at certain times of the year and can do tremendous harm and damage to people and property. So when I hear of a tornado warning in my area, I immediately begin to take authority in the Name of Jesus over my own home and property and over the RHEMA campus. I have a right to take authority over my own home, and, because I'm in charge of the day-to-day operations at the ministry, I have a right to use the Name of Jesus for protection over the ministry property as well.

Also, I never get in an airplane or car to travel anywhere that I don't first appropriate the power of the Name of Jesus. I always say, "In the Name of Jesus, I appropriate the Ninety-First Psalm that says, 'No harm shall come near me; no plague shall overtake me'" (Ps. 91:10).

There have been times when I've sensed in my spirit to wait awhile before leaving for a trip. I'd often find out later that there was a good reason why we were to stay behind that extra ten or fifteen minutes. On one particular occasion, I discovered that if we had left ten minutes earlier, we would have been traveling at the exact place where a major accident occurred at that moment!

So it's important that after you use the Name of Jesus along with confessing the Word, to also follow the leading and unction of the Holy Spirit on the inside — in your spirit.

On another occasion, my wife and I were supposed to leave on a particular morning to fly to a different state for a preaching engagement. The night before we were to leave, I woke up in the middle of the night and sensed fear all around me. So I got up and began to pray. I prayed for two or three hours in Jesus' Name before I got a release, and we carried on our plans as usual. But if I had not gotten that release or note of victory in the Spirit, I wouldn't have boarded that airplane! I don't care about the fact that the tickets were nonrefundable!

"Yes," someone said, "but you were supposed to be at So-and-so's church to preach. You would have been obligated to go no matter what." Maybe so, but I'd rather miss one service and live to preach another one!

Now I'm not going to be dogmatic in saying that plane would have crashed had I not prayed. Some people can allow things like this to get them into fear. There's a difference between yielding to fear, and simply recognizing its presence and giving place to the Holy Spirit to pray about it. That's why it's so important to learn how to follow the leading of the Holy Spirit in your spirit. You also have to know how to use the Name!

> **MARK 16:15-17**
> 15 And he [Jesus] said unto them, Go ye into all the world, and preach the gospel to every creature.
> 16 He that believeth and is baptized shall be saved; but he that believeth not shall be damned.
> 17 And these signs shall follow them that believe; IN MY NAME shall they cast out devils; they shall speak with new tongues.

The literal Greek interpretation of this passage may sound a little strange, but bear with me because it contains a teaching point on the Name of Jesus I want to make. The literal Greek says, "The believing and being baptized will be saved. But the disbelieving will be condemned. Signs and the ones believing these will follow in the Name of Me. Demons, they will expel. Tongues, they will speak with new."

Verse 17 in the *King James Version* says, "*. . . these signs shall follow them that believe; In my* *name . . . .*" Notice the Greek says, "Signs *and* the ones believing; these will follow in the Name of Me." I like the *New International Version* of verse 17. ". . . these signs will ACCOMPANY those who believe: In my name . . . ." In this version, "follow" is translated *accompany*. I like that word. It means *to come alongside*. It helps us better understand the meaning of this scripture.

We have many words in our English language, but often, we have only one word to represent many different meanings, such as our word "love," which can have several different meanings. For example, my wife and I *love* ice cream, but we don't love ice cream in the same manner or to the same degree that we love each other! You can understand what kind of love I'm talking about by the context in which I use the word.

In the Greek, there are different words for our word "love." For example, there's *agape* (the God-kind of love); *phileo* (brotherly love or "friendship" love); and *eros* (intimate, physical love, as between a man and wife).

So when we think of the word "follow" in Mark 16:17, we think of something following *behind* something else. But signs and wonders don't just follow *behind* believers. Various authors of word studies agree that the word "follow" gives the sense of *accompanying.* So signs *come alongside* and *accompany* those believers who know how to use that Name!

Therefore, when you as a believer use the Name of Jesus, you are not alone! Jesus Himself said that signs would accompany you!

You have every right to use the Name of Jesus with confidence! So use that God-given right and use that Name to walk in the victory that God has designed for you. No sickness, disease, lack, demon power, or *any* situation or circumstance can withstand the matchless Name of Jesus! Everything must bow and come under subjection at the mention of that precious Name! There's power in the Name!

---

[1]Smith Wigglesworth, *Ever Increasing Faith*, Springfield, Missouri, Gospel Publishing House.

Chapter 2
The Name Belongs
To the Church

In Chapter 1, I discussed in some detail the power that's in the Name of Jesus. Now I want to talk more about the *authority* that we as believers have in that Name. We need to understand that authority, because the Name of Jesus belongs to us!

In some places in the New Testament, the word "power" is translated in the Greek as *authority*. For example, Jesus said in Luke 10:19, *"Behold, I give unto you POWER to tread on serpents and scorpions, and over all the power of the enemy: and nothing shall by any means hurt you."* This word "power" could also be translated *authority*. We have power and *authority* in the Name of Jesus!

Power of Attorney:
Delegated Power and Authority

Closely connected with the word "authority" is a term that most of us understand in this day and age, the *power of attorney*. Have you ever signed a document or piece of paper that gave someone else the "power of attorney" to act in your behalf in a certain situation? When you give someone power of attorney, you give him or her a legal right to use your name in some type of transaction. It may be the closing of a real-estate deal or the purchase of a car. Power of attorney in those situations means that the person to whom you give authority can legally act on your behalf in those matters.

If you're ever selected to be the guardian of an elderly relative, you will have the power of attorney to handle the affairs of your relative's estate or business dealings. You may have to pay bills in his or her behalf. It's the power of attorney that legally enables you to do that.

In short, "power of attorney" means *a legal right to use a name.* For example, I have no right to use any name except Kenneth W. Hagin. I have no legal right to use your name, and you have no legal right to use my name. Also, no one but the trustees of RHEMA Bible Church (and those whom the trustees designate) have the right to use the name RHEMA Bible Church, Kenneth Hagin Ministries, or RHEMA Bible Training Center. I happen to be one of those trustees, so I have the right or authority to use the name "RHEMA." In order to allow others to use that name, such as RHEMA Bible Training Centre, South Africa, I have to sign legal documents authorizing them to use the RHEMA name.

You see, it has to be done legally or there's no power! It's the same way in the spiritual realm. Power must be delegated legally or that power is null and void. And we have the authority — the power of attorney — to use the Name of Jesus! The Word of God clearly teaches us so. We have the power to use that Name in prayer! We can use that Name in dealing with demons! And we can use that Name in ministering healing!

> **MATTHEW 28:18-20**
> **18 And Jesus came and spake unto them, saying, All power is given unto me in heaven and in earth.**
> **19 Go ye therefore, and teach all nations, baptizing them in the name of the Father, and of the Son, and of the Holy Ghost:**
> **20 Teaching them to observe all things whatsoever I have commanded you: and, lo, I am with you alway, even unto the end of the world. Amen.**

In the first verse of this passage, Jesus says, ". . . *All power is given unto me in heaven and in earth*" (v. 18). If we stop reading right there, someone might say, "That's great! Thank God, Jesus has all authority and power in Heaven and earth. Jesus can do whatever He wants to do, because He has all power."

But there's more to Jesus' statement than just verse 18. Upon saying that all power was given to Him in Heaven and earth, He immediately authorized the Church to go forth into all nations in that power, ". . . *baptizing them in the name of the Father, and of the Son, and of the Holy Ghost"* (v. 19). So the Church has authority too.

You Have Been Authorized To Use the Name!

Look at that same passage in the *New International Version*: "Then Jesus came to them and said, 'All authority in heaven and on earth has been given to me. Therefore go and make disciples . . . .'"

In other words, it seems Jesus was saying, "I have this authority. Now I'm giving it to you. You take it and go make disciples. I am *authorizing* you to do it." Jesus was authorizing the Church to use the authority and power that had been given to Him.

Jesus also said something very important in Matthew 28:20: ". . . *lo, I am with you alway, even unto the end of the world. Amen."* Isn't it wonderful that Jesus is with us? We are not alone. Jesus said that He'd be with us always.

Now notice what Jesus had to say about agreeing in His Name in Matthew 18.

MATTHEW 18:19,20
19 Again I say unto you, That if two of you shall agree on earth as touching any thing that they shall ask, it shall be done for them of my Father which is in heaven.
20 For where two or three are gathered together in my name, THERE AM I in the midst of them.

These verses are wonderful statements of fact from the Word, but many times people take verse 19 out of context and miss the full import of what the Lord is saying. The *New International Version* says, "Again, I tell you that if two of you on earth agree *about anything you ask for*, it will be done for you by my Father in heaven." Certainly, that verse is true, but look again at verse 20 for a clearer meaning.

MATTHEW 18:20 (*NIV*)
20 For where two or three come together in my name, there am I with them.

Many times, people will come together in a service and say, "The Lord is here, because the Bible says that where two or three are gathered together in His Name, He's there."

Well, that's true, but there's more to it than that. You really have to read verses 19 and 20 together to get the full meaning of what's being said: "*. . . if two of you shall agree on earth as touching any thing* *that they shall ask, it shall be done for them of my Father which is in heaven. For where two or three are GATHERED TOGETHER IN MY NAME, there am I IN THE MIDST OF THEM."*

So for the prayer of agreement to be effective, Jesus must be honored in our midst.

That's why Jesus is there, "in the midst of them," when two or three agree in prayer in His Name. He is there to make sure that what was agreed upon comes to pass!

The Power in the Name Is the Power of Jesus Himself!

People don't take much notice at the mention of certain names, because those names carry no weight or authority. But when you mention certain other names, people stop and take notice. Why? Because those names carry authority. There is power behind certain names, even in the natural.

Have you ever watched a policeman directing traffic? He blows a whistle and motions with his hands, and three thousand pounds of automobile will come to a screeching halt! Even forty-thousand-pound trucks yield when a policeman gives the signal. Why? Is it because officer "Billy Smith" is out in the middle of the road directing traffic? No, the name

Billy Smith holds no meaning to those drivers. But the *authority* behind officer Billy Smith does hold meaning! Those drivers will obey the officer's hand signals, regardless of who he is, because of the authority behind him.

Spiritually speaking, the Name of Jesus carries authority in three worlds — in Heaven, on earth, and under the earth! If there were no power or authority in the Name of Jesus — if Jesus were not Deity — then no devil or demon would tremble and bow. But we know that demons do tremble at the mention of the majestic Name of the King of kings and Lord of lords!

Now look again at Matthew chapter 28.

MATTHEW 28:20
20 . . . lo, I am with you alway, even unto the end of the world. Amen.

The secret to the power and authority in Jesus' Name lies in the fact that He is with us! And where Jesus is present, so is His power. He is with us in the power and authority of His Name!

Now back in Matthew 18:20, Jesus said, "When two or three are gathered in My Name, I'm in their midst." How is He in their midst? Of course, Jesus is always present, because He indwells believers by His Spirit. But when believers gather in Jesus' Name,

He is there in their midst *in the power and authority of His Name*! And that's how things get accomplished to the glory of God — in the Name of Jesus!

You see, we don't receive our every need met just because we are born again and Jesus lives in us. No, it's the power and authority in that Name that gets us the things we need and want in life!

Access to the Resources Of Heaven

You know, some people have said that when Jesus gave us authority with the use of His Name, He, in essence, gave us a "signed check." Have you ever had to give someone a signed check? If you have, I'm sure you wanted the person to guard that check with his life! You probably asked him to write the check for the exact amount of the purchase and to return the receipt to you. Why? Because that signed check could be used to withdraw as much money as you had in your checking account!

Well, we have a "signed check"! God has signed it, and, using the Name of Jesus, we can "write our own ticket with God"!

In Jesus' Name, we have access to all the resources of Heaven. Yet too many Christians are trying to be humble, writing out their checks for a dollar! I think the Lord gets upset with us when we don't take advantage of what He's given to us. Someone said, "Well, do you have any Scripture for that?"

Look at Second Kings chapter 13.

2 KINGS 13:14-19 (NIV)
14 Now Elisha was suffering from the illness from which he died. Jehoash king of Israel went down to see him and wept over him. "My father! My father!" he cried. "The chariots and horsemen of Israel!"
15 Elisha said, "Get a bow and some arrows," and he did so.
16 "Take the bow in your hands," he said to the king of Israel. When he had taken it, Elisha put his hands on the king's hands.
17 "Open the east window," he said, and he opened it. "Shoot!" Elisha said, and he shot. "The Lord's arrow of victory, the arrow of victory over Aram!" Elisha declared. "You will completely destroy the Arameans at Aphek."
18 Then he said, "Take the arrows," and the king took them. Elisha told him, "Strike the ground." He struck it three times and stopped.
19 The man of God was angry with him and said, "You should have struck the ground five or six times; then you would have defeated Aram and completely destroyed it. But now you will defeat it only three times."

In this account, King Jehoash wrote his check out too small! Elisha told him to strike the ground with his arrows. So the king struck the ground three times, but the prophet Elisha became angry. Why? Because the king could have struck the ground several more times, but he didn't. Verse 19 in the *New International Version* says, "The man of God was angry with him and said, 'You should have struck the ground five or six times; then you would have defeated Aram and completely destroyed it. But now you will defeat it only three times.'"

Some people think they're being humble when they don't take advantage of everything the Lord has provided for them. They say, "Well, it's not right to think more highly of myself that I ought [Rom. 12:3]. There are others who have greater needs than I have."

Well, it's certainly not right to think more highly of yourself than you ought to think. But what does that have to do with your doing what God has told you to do and appropriating what He says belongs to you?

God has given us vast blessings and benefits in Christ. We might understand it better to say that God has given us a credit card from the bank of Heaven! There are no limits to how much we can be blessed in Him. It's only a matter of our believing and exercising our authority in the earth realm so we can receive those blessings.

Are You Expecting
Little or *Much*?

You see, I think sometimes we don't "strike the ground" enough times, as in the case of King Jehoash. We start out believing God, all right, and we even begin getting blessed a little bit — in a measure. But then we become satisfied with just a little bit, and we quit exercising our faith.

In Second Kings 13 we read that the prophet got upset at the king because the king only struck the ground three times with his arrows. One commentary says that the king may not have thought it was proper to strike the ground with arrows, as a child at play might do. I don't know whether or not that's true, but it's interesting nevertheless that the king didn't ask for or expect enough from God!

Jesus plainly said in John 16 that whatever we asked the Father for in His Name would be granted to us by the Father (John 16:23). Then Jesus said almost the same thing in verse 24.

JOHN 16:24
24 Hitherto have ye asked nothing in my name: ask, and ye shall receive, that your joy may be FULL.

That's one of the reasons Elisha the prophet became upset with King Jehoash: The king stopped short of receiving what was available to him. He didn't ask *fully*. The prophet said to Jehoash, "All right, you only struck the ground three times, so you're only going to defeat the Arameans three times. But if you had struck the ground *five or six* times, you would have utterly destroyed them." In other words, the prophet was saying that if the king had struck the ground some more, he wouldn't have had to deal with the Arameans ever again!

How many times in our own lives do we deal with the same problems, situations, and circumstances over and over again. We get a little bit of victory here and there, so we sort of "ease up." Then before we know it, the devil comes around again to attack us in that same area.

It may be that we didn't "strike the ground" enough times, so we found ourselves in the position of having to continually enforce the enemy's defeat over and over again instead of settling the matter once and for all in that particular area of our lives.

Get hold of this truth! Stand your ground against the devil with the idea in mind of utterly destroying his works in your life! When you utterly destroy something, you don't have to deal with it anymore!

Have you ever noticed that in the Old Testament when the Israelites utterly destroyed some of the cities they went to war against, you never heard of those cities again? When the children of Israel came marching in battle into a certain city, they destroyed everything, and usually, nothing is ever mentioned about that city again.

That's what we need to do to the enemy in our lives to utterly destroy his works. Someone said, "Well now, wait a minute. Let's not overdo it now. There is such a thing as humility."

Yes, there certainly is, and I believe in being humble before God. But I don't believe in being humble before the devil! When God has told us that something belongs to us, we need to act on it! So since He's told us to take the Name of Jesus and use it against poverty, sickness, disease, and so forth, then we need to do it! Actually, doing what God said to do and receiving what He said belonged to us *is* humility.

Some people just want to barely get by, and they call that humility. But if you'll study the Word, you'll find out that God is not talking about our barely getting by; He's talking about our having an abundant supply left over *after* all of our needs are met!

True Humility Always Believes

In the affairs of life, we need to just stay with what the Word says. Doing that would answer so many of our questions and problems. You know, recently, I was looking at one of the old, rare books in our RHEMA campus library. It was a book about tithing and prosperity. The way the author taught, you would have thought he was a contemporary teacher of the Word!

Why is that? Because in the pages of that old book, he was preaching and teaching the unadulterated, unchanging Word of God! Those Bible principles have stood the test of time. Some churches, theologians, and even whole denominations have tried to bury the truth, but the Word of God still stands strong today.

Most of the time when someone comes against the Bible, it's because he's had some kind of bad experience that didn't line up with the Word. He didn't understand why it happened, so, he concocted his own ideas about what happened in order to "explain it away" and soothe his disappointment and confusion.

But I want us to stick with the Word and stand strong for the truths contained in that Book!

Someone said to me, "Hagin, you preach healing strong! You're so dogmatic. But I was in one of your meetings, and I know someone who was there who didn't get healed."

I looked this person right in the eye and said, "That's right. I also preached the New Birth in that meeting, but not everybody got saved either!"

This person replied, "Oh, well, that's *different*."

I said, "No, it's not; it's the same Gospel. It's all there in the same Bible! And I'm not going to quit preaching salvation just because everyone didn't get saved in a particular meeting. That doesn't change the Bible one little bit! I'm not going to quit preaching healing either just because everyone didn't get healed. And I'm not going to quit preaching that God wants to bless us just because everyone's not being blessed!"

Did you know that you can be poor and sick and still go to Heaven? The only prerequisite to going to Heaven is to be saved by the blood of the Lord Jesus Christ. The Bible says, *"For whosoever shall call upon the name of the Lord shall be saved"* (Rom. 10:13). So being healed and blessed is not a requirement to going to Heaven. All you have to do is call upon that Name! But, I'll tell you what — I intend to take advantage of *all* the benefits in Jesus' Name!

If you don't want to take advantage of the benefits that are in the Name, fine. No one can *make* you
receive those blessings. But don't put down others
who are taking advantage of what belongs to them
in Christ.

The Choice Is Yours

The Bible says, *"Bless the Lord, O my soul, and
forget not all his benefits"* (Ps. 103:2). In the natural,
when you become employed by a company, you are
usually told about the benefits that go with the job.
Those benefits may be two weeks' vacation, certain
holidays off with pay, insurance coverage, and so
forth. But I want to tell you something: The company is not going to twist your arm and *make* you
take advantage of their benefits! The benefits have
been provided for you, but *you* have to take advantage of them!

The Lord Jesus Christ Himself said, in effect,
"You have the authority to use My Name, and that
Name will get you the benefits the Word of God
says belongs to you." Now Jesus is not going to
come down here and *force* you to use His Name
and receive His blessings. But the blessings are
still available!

I tell you, anyone who doesn't believe that God wants to bless His people with health and abundant provision has "come too late" to tell me that the blessings are not for us today! I know those blessings belong to us. Many, many times, I have used the wonderful Name of Jesus to march out of tests and trials victoriously! I have used that Name to receive protection in the midst of danger. I've used the Name to command sickness and disease to leave my body and the bodies of my children. And I have used the Name to receive my financial needs met.

I'm not talking about some "way out" something; I'm talking about receiving what the Word promises. And the way to receive is through the Name!

You see, many born-again, Spirit-filled Christians are living at a low level in life. I've run across some of these people. They talk more about what *the devil* is doing than about what *God* is doing. But if they would just get hold of the truth about the Name of Jesus and the power that's in His Name, their lives would be different.

Glorify God, Not the Devil

Back when I was a kid, some churches would have testimony meetings. We had a testimony meeting every week at one of the churches Dad pastored.

Well, I noticed at these meetings that some of the same people would get up to "testify" week after week. They'd always say the same thing. Sister So-and-so would get up and say, "Well, I thank the Lord that I'm saved and sanctified, filled with the Holy Ghost, and on my way to Heaven. You all pray for me; the devil's been after me all day, bless his holy name"!

I'm not telling you something that isn't so! I've heard it! Now that woman didn't mean to praise the devil. She meant to say, "Bless the *Lord's* holy Name." But, as my dad says, she got her praise misplaced!

As a kid, I got tired of hearing people "testify" about one hard-luck story after another. I would often think, *Aren't there some days that are better than others?* I mean, these people weren't living examples of blessed men and women of God!

To this day, I know of ministers who every time you see them have some kind of a hard-luck story to tell. Certainly, they may be going through tests and trials (you can't ignore the facts if you're facing an unpleasant circumstance). But it sometimes gets to the point where I don't even want to ask some of them, "How are you?" because they never talk about the Word of God or about victory. They only talk defeat.

Sometimes I'll get phone calls from ministers. They'll ask me, "How are you doing?" I always answer, "Everything's going well. Praise the Lord." (They don't know that I may be going through a test or trial, but why would I want to brag on the devil and tell what the *devil's* doing? I'd rather talk about what *God* is doing so I can experience victory and deliverance from that test or trial!)

When I say, "Everything's fine," they will say, "Well, I'm glad things are going well for *you*." Then they proceed to tell me things, such as: their bus broke down while they were out of town at a meeting; they had to borrow money to get out of town; they've had throat problems or some other sickness; and so forth.

I am always sincerely sorry when I hear that others are going through difficulties. The difficulties of life come to us all. But, let's turn our talking about the circumstances around. Let's get hold of the Word and talk about what the *Word* has to say so we can believe God for victory and watch those circumstances change!

In other words, we could say, "We had a tough time financially last month, but, thank God, the Word says that God meets every need according to His riches in glory by Christ Jesus! I praise God ahead of time that we're going over the top in Jesus' Name!"

It's all right to recognize the facts and acknowledge your problems. But once you do that, take your stand and declare your victory. Say, "I recognize the facts. But in the Name of Jesus, those facts are going to have to change! Mr. Devil, you're a defeated foe. Now get out of here in Jesus' Name!"

When you start using the Name of Jesus, demons shudder. Their knees start knocking together — because they understand the power of that Name!

Expect a Miracle!

If believers today understood the wealth of power that the Name holds for them, they wouldn't have such low expectations in life. They wouldn't live in such "low places" spiritually. They would take the Name of Jesus and begin to expect God to move. I have always liked the saying that Brother Oral Roberts coined: "Expect a miracle!"

Someone said, "But you can never tell what's going to happen to you."

Yes, I can! I can't stop many of the tests and trials of life that come to us all. But, ultimately, what's going to happen in my life is what I *let* happen based on whether or not I act on God's Word!

For example, the Bible says that I have some power and authority in Jesus' Name. It also says that the Name guarantees that what I'm believing for according to the Word will happen. Now the Bible doesn't say I'm going to walk out of a test or trial in five minutes. It just says that in the Name of Jesus I will receive! So what I want to focus upon is learning about the Name of Jesus and using my authority in that Name!

Faith in the Name

Peter and John understood that the Name of Jesus belonged to them, and they used it on behalf of another who believed in the Name.

ACTS 3:1-7
1   Now Peter and John went up together into the temple at the hour of prayer, being the ninth hour.
2   And a certain man lame from his mother's womb was carried, whom they laid daily at the gate of the temple which is called Beautiful, to ask alms of them that entered into the temple;
3   Who seeing Peter and John about to go into the temple asked an alms.
4   And Peter, fastening his eyes upon him with John, said, Look on us.
5   And he gave heed unto them, expecting to receive something of them.
6   Then Peter said, Silver and gold have I none; but such as I have give I thee: In the name of Jesus Christ of Nazareth rise up and walk.

**7   And he took him by the right hand, and lifted
him up: and immediately his feet and ankle bones
received strength.**

When Peter and John arrived at the Gate called
Beautiful, this poor old man was sitting there all
crippled up. He had no means to make a living for
himself, so he wore the clothes that indicated, "I'm
a beggar," and sat there daily at that same gate.

I want you to notice that Peter said to the lame
man, "I don't have any money, but such as I have —
such as I have — I give unto you." You see, even
though Peter didn't have any money at the time, he
had *something*. What did he have? He had that
Name! And if Peter had it, then we have it, because
we are still under the same covenant. That
covenant hasn't stopped. We're still in the same era,
the same dispensation. It's the Dispensation of
Grace or the Dispensation of the Holy Spirit. We're
still there.

Every believer has the Name of Jesus. He doesn't
even have to be Spirit-filled with the evidence of
speaking in other tongues to have that Name.

Peter had the Name of Jesus. So he said, in
effect, "I don't have any money, man. But what I've
got, I'm going to give you. I've got a Name! In the
Name of Jesus Christ of Nazareth, rise up and
walk!"

Friend, you and I have a Name too. It's a Name that will drive out sickness and disease; a Name that will put poverty on the run; a Name that will set you up above everything; a Name that will put a smile on your face, a song on your lips, a dance in your heart, and a prance in your step!

That Name is ours! It belongs to us!

When you don't have any money, you've got a Name! And that Name will get you some money! When you're sick, you've got a Name! And that Name will get you well! When you're down and out and you don't feel like much of anything, you've got a Name that will pull you out of the doldrums. It will pull you out of depression; it will pull you out of despair and set your feet a-dancin'.

We need to get hold of this! This is the key! It's the key to everything we need in life! We have the right and the privilege to use that Name. All the power that is vested in that Name and all the authority that is given to that Name belongs to us. Glory to God! Hallelujah!

A few years after that incident took place in Acts chapter 3, Peter said to a man who had been bedfast for eight years, "*. . . Aeneas, Jesus Christ maketh thee whole: arise, and make thy bed. And he arose immediately* (Acts 9:34).

Now let me ask you a question. Did the Early Church have a power that we don't have? We are in the same Church Age that started with Peter and the others in the Book of Acts. That was the Early Church. We are the Latter Church, but it's still the same Church Age.

The Early Church "ushered" Jesus out of the world. The Latter Church shall "usher" Him back! No, the Early Church didn't have a power that we don't have. But I think they understood the use of the Name of Jesus better than we do. Thank God for the Word. We need to know the Word in order to make the Name work. But let's don't get so busy thinking only about the Word that we never use the Name.

Now, let me ask you another question. Since we use the Name, why doesn't it seem to do the same today? Why doesn't the Name seem to perform the miracles we saw in the Book of Acts? The answer may be found in Acts chapter 3.

ACTS 3:12,13,16
12 And when Peter saw it, he answered unto the people, Ye men of Israel, why marvel ye at this? or why look ye so earnestly on us, as though by our own power or holiness we had made this man to walk?
13 The God of Abraham, and of Isaac, and of Jacob, the God of our fathers, hath glorified his Son Jesus . . . .

16 AND HIS NAME THROUGH FAITH IN HIS NAME hath made this man strong, whom ye see and know: yea, the faith which is by him hath given him this perfect soundness in the presence of you all.

Why doesn't the Name seem to perform the kind of miracles seen in Acts? Faith in the Name of Jesus! It's not faith in the Word, per se, though you do have to have faith in the Word to have faith in the Name. You've got to believe in the Name! In other words, you need to realize the power in the precious Name of Jesus.

All power is in the Name of Jesus. The Bible explicitly says so. We already read in Matthew 28 that all power or authority was given to Jesus and that He gave that authority to us.

Now look at Mark 16.

MARK 16:15-18 (NIV)
15 He said to them, "Go into all the world and preach the good news to all creation.
16 Whoever believes and is baptized will be saved, but whoever does not believe will be condemned.
17 And these signs will accompany those who believe: IN MY NAME they will drive out demons; they will speak in new tongues;
18 they will pick up snakes with their hands; and when they drink deadly poison, it will not hurt them at all; they will place their hands on sick people, and they will get well."

That's the Great Commission. It all stems from
His Name, and it is carried out in His Name. It's all
in His Name. But, as I said, we've got to have *faith*
in the Name.

> **ACTS 3:16**
> **16 And his name THROUGH FAITH IN HIS NAME
> hath made this man strong . . . .**

In this verse, Peter was rehearsing the healing of
the lame man who sat at the Gate called Beautiful.
Peter was telling people how the man was healed
through his faith in the Name.

This man who was healed had been sitting daily
at the Gate called Beautiful. The gate was right outside the temple area. In fact, Solomon's porch was
just outside the gate. There's every possibility in the
world that the lame man had heard scripture after
scripture read as he sat there begging every day.

There's every possibility that he'd heard the
teaching and the conversation of the rabbis as they
walked by him. There's even a possibility that the
man had heard Jesus speak. But I want you to
notice that it wasn't until the man had faith in the
Name that he received healing. His faith was in
the Name of Jesus, not in the name of Peter or
John or any other disciples.

When the truth of the *power* of the Name really
dawns on our heart, people will be saying of us today,

"There are giants in the land!" Why? Because when we get hold of the truth about what we really have in that Name, we will become a spiritual giant walking through the land, conquering every spiritual foe that raises its head to oppose or hinder us!

Make this your continual confession: "In the Name of Jesus, I'm praying to You, Father, and receiving answers to my prayers that my joy might be complete. In the Name of Jesus, every demon has to flee. In the Name of Jesus, everything that has a name in Heaven, in earth, and under the earth has to bow its knee [Phil. 2:10]."

We can make this confession, not because of who we are, but because of Whose we are! We belong to Jesus! And His Name belongs to us!

Chapter 3
How the Name Came

Some people have a great name because they are born into a family with a great name, such as the royal family of a king. They inherit their name. Some acquire their great name because of something great that they've done, and their names are bestowed upon them. Others obtain their name through conquest.

Sir Francis Drake is one of my ancestors (the relatives on my paternal grandmother's side of the family have the name Drake). Dr. A. M. Drake, my dad's great-grandfather once traced the family tree all the way to England, and Sir Francis Drake is in that lineage.

Francis Drake wasn't always a knight. At one time, he was just a sea captain, but because of all of his accomplishments, the Queen summoned him and gave him his title. He was knighted and became Sir Francis Drake. Actually, the truth of the matter is, he was nothing more than a "pirate" on the high seas! But because England was at war with Spain, and he pillaged the Spanish galleons (he stole their gold), he was knighted by the Queen of England!

Later Sir Francis Drake became a great man in the royal Navy. You see, his great name was acquired through what he'd done — through his accomplishments. The greatness of his name was bestowed upon him.

Almost everyone recognizes the names MacArthur, Eisenhower, and Patton. They were all great military generals. One of them, Dwight D. Eisenhower, became President of the United States. How did their names become great and have such renown? Because of their great accomplishments.

Have you ever heard the names Alvin York and Audie Murphy? Alvin York was one of the most decorated soldiers of World War I, and Audie Murphy was one of the most decorated soldiers of World War II. When my dad pastored in Farmersville, Texas, Audie Murphy was just a kid in that town. But he grew up, went into the armed forces, and by his accomplishments established a great name.

So we see that a great name can be inherited or obtained by bestowal through a person's great accomplishments. With that in mind, I want to show you how Jesus Christ obtained *His* great Name!

By Inheritance

As the Son of God, Jesus inherited His Name, a Name greater than any heavenly being. Notice Hebrews chapter 1.

HEBREWS 1:1-4
1   God, who at sundry times and in divers manners spake in time past unto the fathers by the prophets,
2   Hath in these last days spoken unto us by his Son, whom he hath appointed heir of all things, by whom also he made the worlds;
3   Who being the brightness of his glory, and the express image of his person, and upholding all things by the word of his power, when he had by himself purged our sins, sat down on the right hand of the Majesty on high;
4   Being made so much better than the angels, as he hath BY INHERITANCE obtained a more excellent name than they.

Now look at verse 4 in the *New International Version.*

HEBREWS 1:4 (NIV)
4   So he became as much superior to the angels as the name he has inherited is superior to theirs.

So, first, Jesus got His Name by *inheritance.* God Himself said so through the writer of the Hebrews. The entire discourse in Hebrews chapter 1 sets Jesus apart from any other heavenly being except God Himself.

HEBREWS 1:5,6
5   For unto which of the angels said he at any time, Thou art my Son, this day have I begotten thee? And again, I will be to him a Father, and he shall be to me a Son?

6   And again, when he bringeth in the firstbegotten into the world, he saith, And let all the angels of God worship him.

The Son of God was far superior to any prophet. He was far superior to the heavenly hosts, the messengers of God. Now there was a period of "humiliation" when Jesus the Son was made a little lower than the angels (Ps. 8:5; Heb. 2:7,9), when He took upon Himself the form of human likeness and became a man.

The Bible says Jesus ". . . *made himself of no reputation, and took upon him the form of a servant, and was made in the likeness of men"* (Phil. 2:7). Jesus stripped Himself of His Heavenly glory and took upon Himself the form of man.

As a man, Jesus paid the price and successfully endured all the testings and temptings of humanity so that humanity might be freed from sin. Hebrews 4:15 says, *"For we have not an high priest* [Jesus] *which cannot be touched with the feeling of our infirmities; but was in all points tempted like as we are, yet without sin."* In other words, Jesus did not fail the test!

Then after His resurrection and ascension, Jesus once again assumed His preincarnate position of dignity with the Father. And He was highly exalted far above principalities and angelic hosts (Phil. 2:9).

This more excellent Name that Jesus obtained was obtained, first, by right of inheritance. It is His permanent possession.

In Matthew chapter 1, look at the angel's proclamation that the Savior would be born — that He would come into the earth in human form, taking on a flesh-and-blood body.

> **MATTHEW 1:20,21 (*NIV*)**
> **20 But after he [Joseph] had considered this, an angel of the Lord appeared to him in a dream and said, "Joseph son of David, do not be afraid to take Mary home as your wife, because what is conceived in her is from the Holy Spirit.**
> **21 She will give birth to a son, and you are to give him the name Jesus, because he will save his people from their sins."**

Not only did God work through the Holy Spirit in Jesus' conception, but God was very explicit about what Jesus' Name was to be. There was a reason for that; God had reserved that Name for the individual, His Son, who would receive it by inheritance.

My name is Kenneth Hagin. I received that name at birth. I inherited that name; it was given to me by my father, Kenneth E. Hagin. Well, Jesus inherited the Name "Jesus," because it was the Name given to Him by His Father! Chances are, you have the name you have because it was given to you by *your* father or parent. And just as your earthly father had something to do with your conception, God had something to do with the conception of Jesus. No, it wasn't a natural conception; Mary conceived by the power of the Holy Ghost.

In the natural, a child receives a name by inheritance. Whether good or bad, whatever reputation goes with that name is his inheritance, so to speak. Well, if we're born again, because we're God's children, whatever goes with the Name of Jesus belongs to us — it's our inheritance!

God gave Jesus His Name by inheritance. But then Jesus said, "I'm giving My Church power of attorney to use My inherited Name" (Matt. 28:18,19)!

So Jesus obtained a more excellent Name. It wasn't just any name; it was a *more excellent* Name! Jesus inherited a Name that is better than Gabriel or Michael. Although we know from the Word of God that these two mighty archangels also received their names from God and that they are the chief of all the angels, the Name of Jesus is higher than the name of angels!

HEBREWS 1:4 (*NIV*)
4   So he became as much superior to the angels as the name he has inherited is superior to theirs.

We need to thoroughly understand the authority in the Name of Jesus. We need to understand what took place when Jesus died on the Cross and satisfied all the claims of justice in order to redeem sinful man. Jesus died as our Substitute. Then God in Heaven said, "It is enough" and raised Jesus from the grave. God said to Him, "Thou art My Son. This day have I begotten You [see Ps. 2:7; Acts 13:33; Heb. 1:5; 5:5]. This day have You received the full inheritance of that Name."

In the natural, it is possible for someone not to understand the full meaning and significance of the name they've inherited. Similarly, the significance of the Name of Jesus probably wasn't fully realized or understood until the time of His resurrection from the dead.

Now notice that the Scripture says Jesus not only obtained His Name by inheritance. It also records that God said to Jesus, "Thou art My Son; this day I have begotten thee."

Of this statement Matthew Henry wrote in his commentary:

"You realize that [in Hebrews 1:5,] the writer of Hebrews is going back into the Psalms and picking up a portion of Scripture out of Psalms 2:7. I believe he is. Now this may refer to Jesus' eternal generation or to His resurrection or to His solemn inauguration in the glorious Kingdom at the ascension . . . ."

It is difficult to theologically nail down exactly at what point Jesus inherited His Name. But I believe the Scripture thoroughly corroborates the fact that Jesus Christ the Son of God emptied Himself of the power and glory that He'd had in Heaven with the Father when He came to earth (Phil. 2:6-8). The Word plainly states that Jesus was born a man, a human, and that He lived and gave His life as the Son of Man and the Son of God. Scripture also adamantly supports Jesus' resurrection from the dead and His ascension to the mercy seat of Heaven where He presented His own blood as the atonement for the sins of man (Heb. 9:12).

I personally believe that it was in reference to Jesus' *resurrection* that God the Father made the statement, "You are My Son. This day I have begotten You" (Ps. 2:7; Acts 13:33; Heb. 1:5; 5:5).

Jesus was in Heaven, but He came to earth, taking on the form of man. There has been some debate as to when Jesus was given the Name above every name. Some theologians say it came at His birth. Others say it came at His ascension on High to present His blood on the mercy seat as an atonement. Still others say Jesus' Name was bestowed upon

Him at His resurrection when He arose victorious over death, hell, and the grave!

What we do know positively is that Jesus was given the Name above every name. We have Scripture, God's Word, for it!

PHILIPPIANS 2:9-11
9 Wherefore God also hath highly exalted him, and given him a name which is above every name:
10 That at the name of Jesus every knee should bow, of things in heaven, and things in earth, and things under the earth;
11 And that every tongue should confess that Jesus Christ is Lord, to the glory of God the Father.

Look at this passage in the *New International Version*.

PHILIPPIANS 2:9-11 (*NIV*)
9 Therefore God exalted him to the highest place and gave him the name that is above every name,
10 that at the name of Jesus every knee should bow, in heaven and on earth and under the earth,
11 and every tongue confess that Jesus Christ is Lord, to the glory of God the Father.

Notice in this passage it said Jesus was exalted. This exaltation is consistent with the honor and power of the Name. Jesus had a Name by inheritance, just as many people have a name in this world by inheritance. But there is a certain honor

and exaltation given to Jesus' Name that made His
Name the Name above all names!

By Bestowal

There are several families throughout history
that we could acknowledge as being great, because
they've accumulated much wealth. They are well-
known as a result. People usually take notice of
those who are extremely wealthy, so, in a sense, their
great names are bestowed upon them. Also, if you
mentioned the name of the President of the United
States, every American citizen should recognize that
name. Why? Because there is a certain honor in the
natural that we bestow upon the office of the Chief
Executive of the United States. His position carries
weight and authority.

Jesus' Name was bestowed upon Him, and He
has a Name that is above every name. If something
has a name, Jesus' Name is above that name! In
other words, if you can name it, Jesus is above it! If
it's in Heaven, it has to bow. If it's in the earth, it
has to bow. If it's under the earth, it has to bow to
the Name of Jesus, for He is the King of kings and
Lord of lords and possesses the Name that is above
every name!

But Jesus' Name is more than just a name possessed by some dignitary or person of high-ranking

in society. Jesus' Name really *means* something! And it means something to every man, woman, boy, and girl on the earth.

There is so much significance wrapped up in the Name of Jesus. By way of illustration, when I see the flag of the United States of America, I don't just see red and white stripes and fifty white stars on a background of blue. No, I see what that flag *stands for* — freedom — and I have great respect for that red, white, and blue banner! I'm very proud to have served under those stars and stripes. I'm very proud to have worn the Army green and to have saluted that flag as a serviceman to my country.

And when I hear the national anthem, "The Star-Bangled Banner," I don't just hear a beautiful song. I hear a melody of victory and national pride, combined with a sound of sorrow for the men who died on battlefield after battlefield for the freedom of our great country.

Just as the United States flag has continued to fly "proud and free" through many a conflict, the Name of Jesus is still the Name above all names, even through the smoke and fog of the enemy's battlefield! Jesus is alive and victorious as King of kings and Lord of lords! It doesn't matter what we feel or what's coming or going. At the Name of Jesus, every demon in hell has to fall! At that

Name, every circumstance on earth has to fall! And at that Name, every angelic being has to bow!

You see, the Bible says that God has highly exalted Jesus and has given to Him a Name that's above every name (Phil. 2:9). That means His Name was bestowed upon Him. When somebody *gives* you something, he *bestows* it upon you.

Jesus' Name is the Name above every name. One commentary says that Jesus' Name is a title of dignity and power above all creatures, men, and angels, at which every knee must bow.

The Bible says the whole creation must be subject to Him — things in Heaven, on earth, and under the earth. At the Name of Jesus the inhabitants of Heaven and earth, the living and the dead — all pay homage.

Now, I want you to notice why I believe the bestowal of Jesus' Name as the Name above all names took place in conjunction with His being raised from the dead. Look at Ephesians chapter 1.

EPHESIANS 1:17-21
17 That the God of our Lord Jesus Christ, the Father of glory, may give unto you the spirit of wisdom and revelation in the knowledge of him:
18 The eyes of your understanding being enlightened; that ye may know what is the hope of his calling, and what the riches of the glory of his inheritance in the saints,

19 And what is the exceeding greatness of his power to us-ward who believe, according to the working of his mighty power,
20 Which he wrought in Christ, WHEN HE RAISED HIM FROM THE DEAD, and set him at his own right hand in the heavenly places,
21 Far above all principality, and power, and might, and dominion, AND EVERY NAME THAT IS NAMED, not only in this world, but also in that which is to come.

When Jesus was resurrected from the dead, God set Him above every name that is named (v. 21). Ephesians 1:21 goes right along with Philippians 2:9, which says, *"Wherefore God also hath highly exalted him, and given him a name which is above every name."*

Paul wrote most of the New Testament, and from his writings, we have what is known as the Pauline Revelation. Many times we are taught truths about faith and who we are as new creatures in Christ from the Pauline Revelation. But we haven't heard as much teaching about the authority that is in the Name of Jesus which Paul also brings out in his writings.

EPHESIANS 1:21
21 Far above all principality, and power, and might, and dominion, and every name that is named, not only in this world, but also in that which is to come.

In this verse, Paul was telling us that Jesus'
Name is the Name above every name, not only now,
but in the world to come when He will come again in
glory as the King of kings and Lord of lords (1 Tim.
6:15; Rev. 17:14; 19:16).

> **EPHESIANS 1:21-23**
> **21 Far above all principality, and power, and
> might, and dominion, and every name that is
> named, not only in this world, but also in that
> which is to come:**
> **22 And hath put all things under his feet, and gave
> him to be the head over all things to the church,**
> **23 Which is his body, the fulness of him that filleth
> all in all.**

God not only gave Jesus a Name, He gave Him a
Name to which three worlds must bow — the heavenly world, the earthly world, and the spiritual
"underworld"! That's what Paul was talking about
in these scriptures in Ephesians chapter 1.

Jesus Christ died on the Cross, and because He
consummated God's great plan of redemption, He
has all authority! God set Him *"FAR ABOVE all
principality, and power, and might, and dominion,
and every name that is named, not only in this
world, but also in that which is to come"* (Eph. 1:21).

Through His Name, Jesus has given authority
and power to His Church. That Name is available

to you and I today as believers in the finished work of Christ at Calvary. And that Name will work everywhere, in every situation and circumstance!

By Conquest

We know that Jesus obtained His great Name by inheritance and by bestowal. But He also obtained His Name by *conquest*.

EPHESIANS 1:21
21 Far above all principality, and power, and might, and dominion, and every name that is named, not only in this world, but also in that which is to come.

By His conquest of these principalities, powers, mights, and dominions, Jesus obtained that Name!

I don't know what happened during those three days that Jesus was in the heart of the earth. I do believe that at some point Jesus preached to the spirits in Abraham's bosom, because the Bible refers to that (1 Peter 3:19). There have been many theological arguments over the events that took place during those three days. I don't know that Jesus actually did "mortal combat" with the enemy. We have no record of it, and some theologians want to "nail you to the wall," so to speak, if you say that He did. But there is nothing in Scripture to substantiate that Jesus *didn't* do combat with the enemy, either!

I *do* know that there had to be some kind of contact somewhere, sometime, because it says when Jesus arose from the grave, He had the keys of death, hell, and the grave in His hand. Before that, Satan had them.

I don't know *how* it happened, and I'm not going to get into an argument over it. All I'm glad about is *why* it happened — so that you and I could be free! But let's not get hung up on that. Let's focus on the fact that Jesus did die, that He did rise from the dead, and that He did "spoil principalities and powers." And, that He did it for you and for me!

> **COLOSSIANS 2:15**
> **15 And having spoiled principalities and powers, he made a shew of them openly, TRIUMPHING OVER THEM . . . .**

Another scripture referring to Jesus' victory made the statement that ". . . through death he might bring to nought him that had the power of death, that is, the devil" (Heb. 2:14, *American Standard Version*). Another translation says, "He might paralyse him." We already read that devils and demons tremble at the Name of Jesus (James 2:19). This is also very evident as we study the Gospels and the Acts.

Let's look at the story of the seven sons of Sceva.

> **ACTS 19:13-16**
> **13 Then certain of the vagabond Jews, exorcists, took upon them to call over them which had evil spirits the name of the Lord Jesus, saying, We adjure you by Jesus whom Paul preacheth.**
> **14 And there were seven sons of one Sceva, a Jew, and chief of the priests, which did so.**
> **15 And the evil spirit answered and said, Jesus I know, and Paul I know; but who are ye?**
> **16 And the man in whom the evil spirit was leaped on them, and overcame them, and prevailed against them, so that they fled out of that house naked and wounded.**

These seven brothers, the seven sons of Sceva, had taken it upon themselves to try to exercise authority in the Name of Jesus. Someone had an evil spirit, and the seven brothers said, "*. . . We adjure you by Jesus whom Paul preacheth*" (v. 13). In verse 15 we read that the spirit answered the seven brothers, "*. . . JESUS I know, and PAUL I know, but WHO ARE YE?*"

We can see that the evil spirit had respect for the Name, but, apparently, they didn't have any respect for the seven brothers who were trying to use the Name!

Why did that spirit know Paul? It knew Paul through his authority in the Name of Jesus —

through his power of attorney to use that Name. And, of course, the evil spirit knew Jesus! The spirit knew that Jesus dealt successfully with demons and evil spirits not only in His earth walk but in His death, burial, and resurrection.

That spirit knew Jesus had died on the Cross and that something happened during those three days before He rose again which caused Him to rise victorious over death, hell, and the grave. *Some* sort of conquest took place. I don't know exactly what sort, but Jesus did put to naught principalities and powers, making a show of them openly and triumphing over them (Col. 2:15). The word "naught" means to reduce to nothing. Jesus reduced principalities and powers to nothing!

I've heard people say, "The devil's after me!" Those people aren't walking in the revelation and the reality of what Jesus did in His death, burial, and resurrection. They need to realize that Jesus put the devil to naught, to nothing, and then use their God-given authority over the devil in their own lives. The devil has been reduced to nothing! When you find that out, you'll quit running!

Who's Chasing Who?

Down in Texas, there's a type of little blue snake called a "blue racer." I remember watching my grandma out in her backyard when she'd see one. They were harmless, but as long as Grandma would run from that snake, it would chase her. If she would stop and turn around, facing the snake, the snake would start running from *her*! Then I would have to chase that snake to try to catch it. I had to catch it, because the minute I stopped chasing that snake, it would swing around and start chasing *me*!

That actually happens. As I said, the blue racer is a harmless snake (but it could make you hurt yourself running from it!).

That's what the devil does to a lot of Christians. The devil is a defeated foe; he's been put to naught by Jesus Himself. He can't legally do anything to you — in your own life — that you don't permit him to do (whether it is a permission of consent or a permission of ignorance). But he's chasing Christians around and making them hurt themselves. They need to turn around and put *him* on the run in the Name of Jesus!

The devil is a defeated foe. And with the Name of Jesus, you can enforce his defeat in your own life. Jesus received His Name by *conquest*! Why? Because when you defeat somebody, you conquer him. You gain some kind of conquest.

Jesus came out of that grave with authority over the devil, sin, sickness, disease, poverty, and lack, and He was given the Name above every name. All your authority, all your blessing, and all your answered prayer is wrapped up in the Name of Jesus. That Name will make His conquest a reality in your life. That Name will accomplish whatever you need according to the Word.

Because Jesus received His Name by conquest, the Bible says all things have been put under His feet (1 Cor. 15:25,27; Eph. 1:22; Heb. 2:8).

Do you understand that because of the Name of Jesus, Satan has no right or authority in your life? He has no right to dominate you! It is only when you don't know the truth that he can take advantage of you and dominate you. He will chase you like a Texas blue racer. But when you find out the truth, the truth shall set you free, and you shall be free indeed (John 8:32,36)! The Name of Jesus will put the devil on the run every time!

Power To 'Get the Job Done'

Jesus' Name has the power to get things done. For example, I am the administrative head of Kenneth Hagin Ministries. If someone wanted to get something done at the ministry, he could go from department to department and start throwing my name around, so to speak: "Pastor Hagin wants this done" or "Pastor Hagin wants that done" (even if I don't really want it done!). But a person wouldn't throw my name around if I didn't have any authority. Because of the position I'm in, my name has the power to get certain things done at the ministry.

Similarly, Jesus' Name has the power to get things done — in Heaven, in earth, and under the earth. Because of the position He holds — and because His Name was received by inheritance, bestowal, and conquest — His is the Name that's above every name! At the Name of Jesus, everything that has a name must bow. All of your problems have names; therefore, they must bow to the Name of Jesus. (If you're not shouting about that fact, it's not real to you yet!)

Say this out loud: "Jesus received His Name by inheritance, by bestowal, and by conquest. I have a right to use that Name. By the shed blood of the Lord Jesus Christ, I have power of attorney to use that Name. I'm going to walk forth and shout the Name of Jesus every time the devil raises his head. The devil is under my feet because of the Name of Jesus."

A Psalm

It's a Name that will set you free.
It's a Name that will bring you victory.

It's a Name that will raise you to heights you've never thought of
And take you to places you've never dreamed.
It's a Name that you can use; it belongs to you.
Rejoice, and run to the Lord
In that Name.

Chapter 4
The Name Is the Key

I have a key that unlocks the door of my car. I may say, "I'm going to unlock the door," but, really, it wouldn't be *me* unlocking it. The *key* unlocks the door! I am simply *using* the key!

I may put the key into the ignition and say, "I'm going to start the car." But the key starts the car. I simply insert the key and turn it.

Now I know that on older cars, you can reach under the dashboard and, using the ignition wires, "hot-wire" the car without using a key. But generally speaking, all the power in a car's engine and everything in that car hinges on a little key!

There's a key in the spiritual realm without which we would get nowhere in life. That key unlocks the windows, doors, and storehouses of Heaven. It unlocks the power from on High! The "key" is His Name — the Name of Jesus! Jesus is the Mediator, the Intercessor, the Advocate, the Lord who stands between us and the Father. And He's given us His Name.

The Scripture has something to say concerning the Name of Jesus as the key. In Jesus' death, burial, and resurrection, He obtained the key to our spiritual authority. Then He gave *us* the key. He gave us the authority to do His works in His Name.

When Jesus appeared to John on the isle of Patmos, He said, *"I am he that liveth, and was dead; and, behold, I am alive for evermore, Amen; and have the KEYS of hell and of death"* (Rev. 1:18).

> **REVELATION 1:18 (*NIV*)**
> **18 I am the Living One; I was dead, and behold I am alive for ever and ever! And I hold the keys of death and Hades.**

As I said in the previous chapter, I don't know exactly what happened during that three-day span after Jesus' crucifixion when He was out of His body. Some people get upset at you if you say that Jesus had a conflict with the devil. But at some time during those three days, Jesus had to have met the devil, because Jesus came back with the keys that the devil had previously.

Where the Word says that Jesus had possession of "the keys of hell and of death," it is not talking about death as the cessation of life. It's talking about *spiritual death*. The last enemy that's going to be put underfoot (it hasn't happened yet) is the cessation of life, which is natural death (1 Cor. 15:26). So in Revelation 1:18, Jesus was talking about holding the keys of *spiritual* death. In other words, through Him, spiritual death could no longer have dominion over those who accepted Jesus as Savior and received eternal life.

The Key to Spiritual Authority

Do you realize that the one who holds the key has the authority? By way of illustration, I have a key in my possession that can unlock every lock on our ministry campus. It's called the grand-master key. I have that key, and I have authority to use it anytime.

But my authority extends beyond that. I have authority to say which persons can use the key, and I have the authority to give a copy of the key to whomever I please. In other words, I have authority to use the key, and I have authority to *delegate* authority to use the key.

We know that Jesus has all power and authority in Heaven and earth (Matt. 28:18). But what did Jesus do when He conquered the enemy? He gave *you* the key. He delegated authority to you. He gave the "key" to us, His Church. What is the key? The key is the *Name*!

> **MARK 16:17,18**
> **17 And these signs shall follow them that believe; IN MY NAME shall they cast out devils; they shall speak with new tongues.**

18 They shall take up serpents; and if they drink any deadly thing, it shall not hurt them; they shall lay hands on the sick, and they shall recover.

We have authority *in His Name.* What are we commanded to do in that Name? Cast out devils, heal the sick, and receive whatever the Word promises us. The power to do these things is in the authority that's in the Name — the Name is recognized in three worlds.

At the Name of Jesus, angels stand at attention; humanity falls on its face; and demons tremble like a leaf in the wind.

Why do people bow to or reverence the Name of Jesus? Why do angels reverence and recognize that holy Name? Why do demons shudder in fear? Because Jesus was given a Name that's above every Name, and at that Name, *every* knee shall bow!

Our Authority Is Still in Force Today

Some people say that healing has been done away with. They say that tongues have been done away with and that the Church doesn't have any authority. Now let me ask you a question. If that is so, then what is the use in obeying Matthew 28:19, which says, "Go ye therefore"? What is the use of carrying a key around in your pocket if that key is useless — if it doesn't unlock anything?

When I leave town by plane, none of the keys I ordinarily carry are of any use to me. I take them out of my pocket and put them in my briefcase, because it wouldn't do any good to carry them while I'm in another city. Why should I clutter my pocket with a "useless" set of keys, since there aren't any keys on my key ring that would unlock anything in the city I'm visiting?

For example, I could fly to Atlanta from Tulsa and find a car identical to the one I own. It could be the same make, model, year, and even the same color. But my car key will not work on that car. My key is useless as far as that other car is concerned.

So if the Church doesn't have any spiritual authority today, as some people claim, then those keys that Jesus retrieved are useless, and He wasted His time telling us to "go ye therefore" in His Name!

But, no! The Name of Jesus works anytime, anywhere! We have authority in that Name!

Have you ever carried around a key, the purpose of which you completely forgot? I mean, you forgot what lock or door it was intended to unlock? I was looking through my key ring awhile back, and as I noticed one particular key, I asked my wife, "What in the world is this key for? I'm going to take this key off my key ring."

She said, "No, don't take it off. If you do, don't throw it away. Somebody gave it to you for a reason or you wouldn't have it on your ring."

Then we figured out what the key was for. It was for RHEMA Ranch, an off-campus campsite and retreat facility owned and operated by the ministry. I hadn't been down there in a while, so I'd forgotten all about it. I'm sure glad I didn't throw that key away! I would have needed it sooner or later, and I didn't want to be without it.

We have the Name of Jesus, and the Name is the key to the spiritual authority that we possess in Him. The Name is unlike any other key you own, so make sure to hold on to the Name wherever you go, because, as I said, that key works anytime, anywhere.

The authority in the Name of Jesus hasn't been done away with. There *is* still salvation; there *is* healing; there *is* prosperity; there *is* the power of the Holy Spirit and speaking in tongues. We just saw in Mark 16 that one of the signs that shall follow the Name is "they shall speak with new tongues" (v. 17).

The Name Is the Key to Signs and Wonders

Look again at Mark 16:17: "*. . . these signs shall FOLLOW them that believe; In my name shall they cast out devils; they shall speak with new tongues.*" You could say that another way: "These signs shall *accompany* the believing one."

Let's look at that word "accompany" again. As I pointed out in chapter 1, if someone accompanies you somewhere, he or she *goes along with you.* Well, the signs listed in Mark 16 *go along with* the believing one in the Name of Jesus.

As I also pointed out in the first chapter, many still say, "Yes, but that's talking about the Early Church. That Name belonged to the Early Church." Yes, but it also belongs to the Church today. Otherwise, what are you going to do with Acts 4:12?

ACTS 4:12
12 Neither IS there salvation in any other: for there IS NONE OTHER NAME under heaven given among men, whereby we must be saved.

The Name of Jesus belongs to us today; in fact, there is no other Name under Heaven given by which a person can be saved.

The Name of Jesus still has all the power that it ever had. And there's more to the Name of Jesus than our salvation. The Name of Jesus encompasses, enwraps, and encircles all of the majesty, power, and glory that it has ever had from time immemorial.

God lifted Jesus up and exalted Him when He raised Him from the dead victorious over death and hell. The Father God exalted Jesus to the highest position in the universe or anywhere. Now Jesus is seated at the right hand of the Father, far above all

other authorities and powers. God conferred upon
Jesus the highest Name in three worlds. Jesus, in
His resurrected body, is seated physically at the right
hand of the Father. But Jesus left us His Name. His
Name with all its power, authority, might, dominion,
and dignity is yours and mine today!

J-e-s-u-s. The sound of that majestic Name
reverberates with power and brings the tangible
Presence of God on the scene. When I say "Jesus," I
want to cry, laugh, shout, dance, and bow down —
all at the same time! That Name evokes this kind of
emotion. It evokes in me a tremendous desire to
honor Him, the King of kings. It also evokes in me
the confidence to be able to go out and conquer situations and circumstances in life.

Spiritual Authority Carries Weight

Jesus never walked in defeat on the earth in His
ministry. He never found Himself without the power
to heal or deliver because the *Name* stands for the
Person. And Jesus was the Son of God.

Sometimes my son, Craig, who is Operations
Manager of Kenneth Hagin Ministries, will call me
to relay a message from my dad, Brother Hagin.
Craig will say, "PaPa wants you to do such-and-
such." Brother Hagin may not physically be present,
but his authority is in his name and so I do such-
and-such.

If a coworker walked up to you and said, "Your boss wanted you to do a certain thing," would that order carry any authority or weight as far as you're concerned? Would you obey your boss or just go about your business doing what you wanted to do? No, if you're smart, you'd carry out your boss's orders, because the authority of his name compels you to obey him. Why? Because he or she is the one in charge at your workplace!

Well, Jesus Christ is in charge! And the Name stands for the Person. The Name stands for the honor. The Name stands for the glory. The Name stands for the authority. The Name stands for the power that is vested in that Name. And that Name, Jesus, is mine and yours to use, because He said, ". . . *All power is given unto me in heaven and in earth. Go ye therefore, and teach all nations, baptizing them in the name of the Father, and of the Son, and of the Holy Ghost*" (Matt. 28:18,19).

The Name Is Our Inheritance

When Jesus gave authority to His Church — the ecclesia, His called-out ones — He gave us a rich inheritance along with the use of His Name!

If we could just grasp the idea that the devil has been stripped of his power and that we have been given the authority to use the Name of the

One who defeated him! Jesus stripped the enemy
of all power — of power to hurt, harm, inflict disease, and destroy. And all we have to do to *enforce*
the enemy's defeat is to use the Name!

In His earthly ministry, Jesus was our Example. He showed us how to use spiritual authority.

> **MATTHEW 8:5,6**
> **5 And when Jesus was entered into Capernaum,
> there came unto him a centurion, beseeching him,
> 6 And saying, Lord, my servant lieth at home sick
> of the palsy, grievously tormented.**

In the *New International Version*, these verses
read, "When Jesus had entered into Capernaum, a
centurion came to him, asking for help. 'Lord,' he
said, 'my servant's home paralyzed and in terrible
suffering.'"

Jesus said, "I will come and heal him" (v. 7).

> **MATTHEW 8:8-10**
> **8 The centurion answered and said, Lord, I am
> not worthy that thou shouldest come under my
> roof: but speak the word only, and my servant
> shall be healed.
> 9 For I am a man under authority, having sol-
> diers under me: and I say to this man, Go, and he
> goeth; and to another, Come, and he cometh; and
> to my servant, Do this, and he doeth it.
> 10 When Jesus heard it, he marvelled, and said to
> them that followed, Verily I say unto you, I have
> not found so great faith, no, not in Israel.**

Verse 10 says, *"When Jesus heard it, he marvelled . . . ."* Why did He marvel at what the centurion said? Because the centurion understood authority. He understood the power of the word of someone speaking with authority.

But the centurion also understood Jesus' spiritual authority. The centurion understood that Jesus was Master over disease, demons, and the laws of nature. He understood that Jesus had authority over sickness, disease, demons, and devils! Throughout the Gospels we read that they obeyed Him when He spoke. He had authority over them. And this centurion understood that. So he knew that all Jesus had to do was to say the word!

Get hold of that! The reason the centurion urged Jesus to just say the word was that he, too, was a man in authority. He had authority over a hundred soldiers in his company. So he told Jesus, *"For I am a man under authority, having soldiers under me: and I say to this man, Go, and he goeth; and to another, Come, and he cometh; and to my servant, Do this, and he doeth it"* (v. 9).

In other words, the centurion was telling Jesus, "I understand the power of authority, and I recognize Your authority. All You have to do is say the word, much like I do when I am commanding my soldiers. When I speak to my men, they must obey.

When You speak to sickness and disease, they must obey. You have been set in authority over all the laws of nature, over all demons, over all sickness, over all disease — over everything! All You have to do is speak!"

In one situation, Jesus did say to the wind and the waves, "Peace. Be still. Winds, cease." And the boisterous sea became as calm and smooth as glass (Mark 4:39). Why could Jesus do that? Because He had the authority! And He said, "Through My Name, I give that authority to My Church."

We Are To 'Speak The Word Only'!

How do *we* exercise the authority Jesus gave us in His Name? We have to say something! We have to "speak the word only"! We have to say, "In the Name of Jesus, I have the victory. In the Name of Jesus, every demon, every sickness, every bit of poverty, and anything with a name that's hindering me has to flee, because it is all under the authority of the Name that's above every name!"

The Church has possession of that Name. I'm not talking about your church or my church; I'm talking about the Church of the Lord Jesus Christ. Those who are born again by the blood of Jesus — *they* have that authority. They have the power in Jesus' Name. He gave it to us. He gave us the key.

ACTS 3:1-6 (*NIV*)
1 One day Peter and John were going up to the temple at the time of prayer—at three in the afternoon.
2 Now a man crippled from birth was being carried to the temple gate called Beautiful, where he was put every day to beg from those going into the temple courts.
3 When he saw Peter and John about to enter, he asked them for money.
4 Peter looked straight at him, as did John. Then Peter said, "Look at us!"
5 So the man gave them his attention, expecting to get something from them.
6 Then Peter said, "Silver or gold I do not have, but what I have I give you. In the name of Jesus Christ of Nazareth, walk."

Notice in verse 6, Peter says, ". . . *what I have* I give you." You can't give something to someone that you don't have! The same is true with Jesus' authority. He couldn't give it away to the Church if He didn't possess it Himself. But the Bible clearly states that He did give it to us, His Church. And that He sent us as His delegates and representatives throughout the world to do His works *in His Name.*

That's what Jesus did when He gave us His Name. He said, "I still have all My power and all My authority, and I sit at the right hand of the Father, but I'm giving you the key. I'm giving you My Name. You possess it; it belongs to you. Now go use it. Use what I have given you."

But most Christians in the Church today don't understand the power and authority that's in the Name. They don't understand that they have a right to use that Name. Nevertheless, every person who's been born again by the blood of the Lord Jesus Christ has that Name and can use it. You don't even have to be baptized in the Holy Spirit with the evidence of speaking in other tongues to use that Name.

An Unrenewed Attitude Will
Short-Circuit the Power of the Name

That Name is for every born-again child of God. Yet the attitude of many in the church world is, *Help me, Lord, to hold out till the end. Jesus, come quickly. The devil's taking over everything, and He's stronger than the Church.*

To listen to some Christians talk, you'd think we've been left orphans, hopeless and helpless. They have a "poor ole me" attitude and say things, such as, "I can't ever get anything from the Lord. Pray for me that I'll hold out faithful to the end. But I don't know whether I will or not; I *hope* so."

That's not New Testament Christianity! New Testament Christianity is expressed in First John 4:4: *". . . greater is he that is in you, than he that is in the world."*

Who is in you? The Spirit of Jesus Christ. What do you have because His Spirit is in you? You have authority; you have a right to use His Name!

The Name is the key. Or we could say it like this: The key to our spiritual authority is in the Name. And the following scriptures relate who we are in Jesus and who He is to us because of the Name.

> **ROMANS 8:37**
> **37 Nay, in all these things we are more than conquerors through him that loved us.**
> **HEBREWS 13:5,6**
> **5 . . . I will never leave thee, nor forsake thee.**
> **6 So that we may boldly say, The Lord is my helper, and I will not fear what man shall do unto me.**

But many of us have defeated and have robbed ourselves of many blessings that should be ours. There are three main reasons for this: 1) We've failed to understand the power and the purpose in the Name of Jesus. 2) We've failed to realize that the Name belongs to us. 3) And we've failed to appropriate that Name for ourselves, acting on the authority that we've been given.

Spiritual Authority Can Be
Of No Avail if It Is Not Appropriated

Charles Hadden Spurgeon, a great English preacher, tells of being invited to a little shanty once to minister to an old woman who was reported to be dying of malnutrition. Her physical life was in danger. So someone had asked Rev. Spurgeon to visit her.

In her tiny, beat-up house, Rev. Spurgeon said he noticed a document hanging on the wall and recognized it as an official, legal document. He asked the dying woman, "Is this yours?"

"Yes," the woman replied, "I worked as a maid in the household of Lady So-and-so for nearly fifty years. She gave me this just before she died. I've been so proud of it that I framed it. It's been hanging on that wall for the past ten years, ever since she passed away."

Spurgeon asked, "Would you allow me to take this and have it examined?"

"Oh, yes, but please don't lose it," the woman replied. "It means so much to me." So Spurgeon took the document to the authorities to have it read more carefully.

You see, this woman had been born into a very poor family and had worked hard all her life. She never got an education and didn't know how to read. Many people in the "lower caste" of society in the mid- to late-1800's were in her situation. They simply didn't have the same opportunities as those who were more well-off financially.

When Spurgeon presented the document to the authorities, they asked him, "Where did you get this? We've been looking for this. It is a bequest."

You see, this English noblewoman had left her maid a home and enough money to live on for the rest of her life! Yet that woman had continued to live in that one-room shanty made out of wooden crates. She was starving to death, while hanging on her wall was enough money to buy food and all the finery she could have possibly wanted! And that money had been gathering interest all those years!

Spurgeon helped that woman get her inheritance, but it didn't do her as much good as it would have had she known earlier what the document, that she treasured so dearly, really meant.

I want you to understand that in the Word of God, you have a "document"! It tells you what belongs to you. It tells you about the Name of Jesus. But just like the woman who hung her prized document on the wall, some Christians "cherish" their Bible — the Book itself — to the point at which they're afraid to use it. They won't turn its pages, much less study its words and mark its passages. They just let their "treasure" sit on a coffee table or shelf.

Peter knew what he had in the Name of Jesus. In the Name of Jesus, he had the authority to tell a crippled man to "rise and walk." At the Gate called Beautiful, Peter said to the lame man, ". . . *such as I have give I thee: In the name of Jesus Christ of Nazareth rise up and walk*" (Acts 3:6)!

It's time that we as the Church of the Lord Jesus Christ wake up! It's time that we begin to realize what we hold in our hands. It's time for us to march out like Peter and do the works of Jesus. Peter understood what he had — the Name of Jesus Christ of Nazareth! I want you to notice that he didn't say, "In the Name of the *Church*, rise and walk." He *didn't* say, "In the name of the *prophet or preacher*." He didn't say, "In the name of the *Law*." No, Peter said, "In the Name of *Jesus*, rise and walk"!

I thank God for this legal document of the New Covenant, the New Testament. It's sealed by the blood of the Lord Jesus Christ. Jesus went away and now sits at the right hand of the Father, but He left us His Name. In that Name is vested all power, glory, and majesty.

Now it's up to you to do something with the Name of Jesus. The Name is the key that will set you free. It will give you that which you long for. Don't let the Word of God or the Name of Jesus "hang on a wall or lie on a table." Pick it up and begin to march forward to receive what belongs to you!

Chapter 5
The Majesty of the Name

Who Is Jesus?

Now let's take a look in this chapter at the majesty of Jesus' Name.

Who is this Jesus, whose Name holds such power? Many *think* they have the answer. Doctrines of other religions present such ideas as, "Jesus was a human man who demonstrated Christ." Or "Jesus Christ Himself was nothing more than a medium of high order."

Some groups claim, "Jesus Christ, a created individual, is the second greatest personage of the universe, the first and only direct creation by his Father, Jehovah." Other groups say, "Jesus Christ is Jehovah, the first-born among spirits of the children of Elohim, to whom all others are juniors."

Many modern theologians say, "Jesus was a man so good, his deluded followers took him for a god. Jesus was divine in the same sense that all are divine."

These false ideas about Jesus Christ, the Savior of mankind and everlasting Son of the Living God, are nothing more than ideas of man and doctrines of devils. But what does *God's Word* say? Who is Jesus?

JOHN 1:1,14
1   In the beginning was the Word, and the Word was with God, and the Word was God ....
14 And the Word [Jesus] was made flesh, and dwelt among us, (and we beheld his glory, the glory as of the only begotten of the Father,) full of grace and truth.

That's who Jesus is!

Did you know that in modern times, controversy rages among various religious organizations and denominations about whether or not Jesus is really deity? In fact, some denominations have publicly stated that they don't really know whether or not Jesus was the Son of God! Others deny the Virgin Birth. I'm talking about major denominations that were originally built and established upon those fundamental beliefs!

A leader in one of the larger denominations wrote an article, stating, in effect, "After nearly fifty years in the ministry, I no longer believe in the virgin birth of Jesus Christ. I've come to the conclusion that you don't have to believe in the deity of Christ [to be saved]. I'm not going to discuss it, but I will say that I do not know whether Jesus was the Son of God or not."

When people get to the point where they are questioning basic elemental truths from Scripture and the deity of the Lord Jesus Christ, the Name of Jesus means nothing to them. If Jesus was not virgin-born and if He is not deity, then He is not God. And if He is not God come in the flesh, His Name holds no meaning or significance in spiritual matters.

The deity of Jesus, the incarnation of the Son of God in human flesh, is the anchor of all Christianity. So if these things are not true, we have lost the very heart of the message; there is nothing left.

However, it *is* true that Jesus Christ is the Son of God who was born of a virgin, taking upon Himself human flesh, human likeness! He came to this earth, lived, and died a cruel death on the Cross of Calvary as our Substitute. According to God's own plan to redeem us, Jesus shed His blood so that those who would believe on Him could be saved and receive eternal life through Him.

The effects of these controversies that challenge the Virgin Birth and the deity of Christ are felt in our world today in a lawlessness of society that didn't exist in years gone by. We would be considered fools if we didn't at least recognize that crime is sweeping our country in unprecedented measures.

But that is not surprising in light of the fact that many have tried to take the heart of the

Christian message, which people have believed and adhered to for years, and "rip it to shreds." Apart from Christ and Christianity, man has nothing left but fending for himself in life without God. And that condition can breed every kind of illicit act imaginable (plus many that are *not* imaginable!).

You can't believe in the deity of the Lord Jesus Christ and live a promiscuous life. You can't believe in the deity of the Lord Jesus Christ and intentionally harm your brother.

You see, if Jesus isn't God come in the flesh, then there's no use to follow His example or His precepts. There's no use following the morals of the Word of God. There's no use following only business dealings that are moral and upstanding.

Every individual on the face of the earth has to answer the question, "Is Jesus deity, or was He just a man?"

Jesus Christ *is* deity; He *is* the Son of God, the Savior of the world. There's no disputing those facts if you believe that the Bible is the holy, infallible Word of God. And it *is*. God has given us His Word to live by. It's an imperishable and unchanging guide that we can stand on, adhere to, and trust unwaveringly amid the uncertainties of life.

But no one can *make* a person believe something. The decision to believe belongs to each human being separately. Each man, woman, boy, and girl must make the choice in his or her own heart. Because the Bible says that all must stand before the Judgment Seat of Christ (2 Cor. 5:10).

The problem is, when people don't believe in the deity of Christ, they usually don't believe the rest of the Bible either. Therefore, they follow their own impulses, instincts, and devices along the road of life. Many live by the popular saying of the '60s and '70s, "Do what you want to do. It's okay as long as it doesn't hurt anybody."

Without a person's knowledge of Jesus as Savior and of the power of the indwelling Holy Spirit, he will lose in the fight to live holy and without sin. The Bible says that our own righteousness, apart from the righteousness that God imparts, is as filthy rags (Isa. 64:6).

You must understand that Jesus Christ is deity. He is the One of whom the Apostle John said "was made flesh and dwelt among us" (John 1:1). Jesus is the Son of God. He was God manifested in the flesh. He is the Way, the Truth, and the Life (John 14:6). He is alive today, and His Name means something!

If there is no *deity* in the Name of Jesus, then there's no *authority* in the Name either, and no devil is going to bow. But we know what the Word of God says — at that Name, everything in Heaven, in earth, and under the earth comes to attention and bows its knee (Phil. 2:9).

When anyone came into the presence of royalty in Old Testament times when countries were governed by kings and queens, they would bow. When someone bowed, he was not bowing to a king or queen as an *individual*; he was bowing and showing reverence or respect for the power behind that king or queen.

When I come to attention and salute the stars and stripes represented on the flag of the United States of America, I know that I'm standing at attention before a piece of cloth. But what am I really saluting? A piece of cloth? No! I'm saluting what that cloth stands for. All the power of the United States government is behind that flag. The American flag represents our freedom and the men and women who gave their lives so our flag could fly high and proud.

We don't pay a lot of attention to flags here in America. But if you were in a foreign country and got into trouble, you'd start looking for the building displaying that flag! Why? Because if you can get inside the doors of the United States embassy, the laws of that foreign nation can't touch you! Behind the doors where our flag flies, an American citizen can find asylum and immunity from unjust laws and accusations.

U.S. Marines are stationed on guard at the gates of our embassies overseas. Your U.S. passport will grant you entrance, but if you were being chased, for example, those marines wouldn't let anyone else through. The only way your pursuers could get to you is through the legal process of the U.S. government — they have to submit to the power behind the flag that flies over the top of that embassy.

We need to understand the power in the Name. That Name is backed by deity. The Name of Jesus is a strong tower (Ps. 61:3; Prov. 18:10). When you run to Him, you are safe! When you run to Jesus and are trusting Him, the only way the devil can get to you is through the Name. The devil has to go through Jesus to get to you!

But the devil doesn't want to come through that Name. He's already dealt with that Name once, and he got whipped! Jesus died and was put in the grave, but death couldn't hold Him there. The deity and power of Almighty God raised Him. And now all the power of Heaven is in the Name of Jesus!

If we are ever going to accomplish what we need to accomplish, we are going to have to understand the deity and the power that is behind the Name.

Salvation in the Name

In the Name of Jesus there is power. In that Name, there is salvation. *There is no salvation apart from the Name of Jesus.*

> **MATTHEW 1:21,23**
> **21 And she [Mary] shall bring forth a son, and THOU SHALT CALL HIS NAME JESUS: for HE SHALL SAVE HIS PEOPLE FROM THEIR SINS....**
> **23 Behold, a virgin shall be with child, and shall bring forth a son, and they shall call his name Emmanuel, which being interpreted is, God with us.**

> **ACTS 4:11,12**
> **11 This is the stone which was set at nought of you builders, which is become the head of the corner [Jesus Christ].**
> **12 Neither is there salvation in any other: for there is none other name under heaven given among men, whereby we must be saved.**

You can't come to God any other way except through the Name of Jesus. Some people say, "Well, you know, you can look at nature and see God." Sure, that's a fact! I mean, all you have to do is look around to see beautiful flowers and the majestic sky. All you have to do is hear the birds sing to realize that there's something behind all of this creation of beauty. You can look at many places on earth and see God in the beauty of those places. But to *know* God and be in fellowship with Him, you must come through Jesus Christ.

Some people say, "Well, you're narrowing it down too much. You're not giving everyone a chance by saying there's only one way. Open it up a little so others can make it to Heaven who don't want to believe that way."

I didn't write the Bible, and I didn't make the rules. *God* did. And He said, "*. . . there is none other name under heaven given among men, whereby we must be saved*" (Acts 4:12). What was He saying? He was saying that there is no other Name but the Name of Jesus by which men and women can be saved!

Jesus said something similar in John 14.

JOHN 14:6
6   Jesus saith unto him, I am the way, the truth, and the life: no man cometh unto the Father, but by me.

Many people say, "I believe that if you're a good person and do good works, you'll be all right; you'll go to Heaven." Well, thank God that there are those who are endeavoring to be good people, but we aren't saved by being good.

Being a good person doesn't save you. Joining a church doesn't save you. Just *going* to church doesn't save you. What saves you is coming to Jesus and receiving God's forgiveness in the Name of Jesus (Acts 2:38; 10:43). That's what the Bible says. Jesus is the Way — the *only* Way. There is no other way to Heaven except through Jesus. There is no other way to eternal life except through that Name! (I'll talk more about salvation and the Name of Jesus in another chapter.)

Three Baptisms

The Name of Jesus is not only involved in salvation, it is also involved in baptisms. A person is saved through the Name of Jesus, and the believer is baptized in the Holy Spirit through the Name of Jesus. Look at what Matthew and Acts has to say about this.

> **MATTHEW 28:19**
> **19 Go ye therefore, and teach all nations, baptizing them in the name of the Father, and of the Son, and of the Holy Ghost.**

> **ACTS 2:38**
> **38 Then Peter said unto them, Repent, and be baptized every one of you in the name of Jesus Christ for the remission of sins, AND YE SHALL RECEIVE THE GIFT OF THE HOLY GHOST.**

You could say it like this: There are three baptisms. *First* is the baptism into the Body of Christ in the New Birth.

1 CORINTHIANS 12:13a
13 For by one Spirit are we all baptized into one body....

The *second baptism* is the baptism in water, signifying the believer's break with the world and his being raised to a new life in Christ.

The *third baptism* is the baptism in the Holy Spirit with the evidence of speaking in other tongues. I will explain all three of these baptisms according to Scripture later in this chapter.

Hebrews 6 has something to say about there being more than one baptism.

HEBREWS 6:1,2 (NIV)
1 Therefore let us leave the elementary teachings about Christ and go on to maturity, not laying again the foundation of repentance from acts that lead to death, and of faith in God,
2 instruction about baptisms, the laying on of hands, the resurrection of the dead, and eternal judgment.

The writer of Hebrews says, "instruction about baptism*s*." That's plural, so we know there is more than one baptism. Some people will immediately object and refer to Ephesians 4:4 and 5, which says, *"There is one body, and one Spirit, even as ye are called in one hope of your calling; One Lord, one faith, one baptism."*

But there is no contradiction here, because in the context of Ephesians chapter 4, Paul was talking about salvation. You can read the context of that scripture and understand that Paul was talking about salvation. There is only one baptism into Christ, which is the New Birth.

But in Hebrews, the writer isn't talking just about salvation. He is talking about "the foundation that's already been laid." Then he tells us in Hebrews 6:2 what that foundation is: *instructions about baptisms, the laying on of hands, the resurrection of the dead,* and *eternal judgment.* The writer was talking about the overall picture, not just salvation, as I said, which is the subject of Ephesians 4:5.

"Baptism" means *to immerse; to put into.* For example, when someone is born again, he is *put into* the Body of Christ.

1 CORINTHIANS 12:13 (*NIV*)
13 For we were all baptized by one Spirit into one body . . . .

What body? *The Body of Christ!* Now the Body of Christ is not the local church. The local church is a *part* of the Body of Christ. The Body of Christ in the Word of God is known as the "ecclesia," the *called out ones* or those who have been born again.

Each local church is its own local body or entity, but each local church is a part of the overall Body of Christ. And each local church member is a member of the Body of Christ.

Now in the natural, a body has a head. So spiritually, Jesus is the Head, and we as Christians are the Body.

The head of a person doesn't go by one name and the body by another name! No, the head and the body go by the same name. For example, my name is Kenneth Wayne Hagin. My head doesn't go by Kenneth and my body go by John! Every part of me is Kenneth!

The First Baptism:
Baptism Into the Body of Christ

The first baptism we are baptized into is the Body of Christ. So once we are immersed, or put into Christ's Body, we are the Body, and He is the Head.

GALATIANS 3:27,28
27 For as many of you as have been baptized into Christ have PUT ON CHRIST.

28 There is neither Jew nor Greek, there is neither bond nor free, there is neither male nor female: for ye are all one in Christ Jesus.

Verse 27 is talking about being born again.

The Second Baptism: Water Baptism

The second baptism that I referred to is water baptism. Water baptism will not save. A believer is baptized in water *after* he's been put or baptized into the Body of Christ through the New Birth. Being baptized in water is simply an outward expression of an inward act. It's the outward evidence of what has happened inwardly through the New Birth. When you're put into the water, it signifies that you've been put into the Body of Christ. Then when you are raised up out of the water, it signifies that all things have become new and old things have been left behind. You have been raised to a new life with Him!

You're probably familiar with my father's experience of being bedfast and on his deathbed as a sixteen-year-old boy. Before he was healed, he had an out-of-body experience. In other words, his spirit left his body, and he descended into the pits of hell (he hadn't been born again yet). And as he was descending, he began to holler out, "Lord! I've been baptized in water! Lord, I belong to the church!"

What Dad was trying to say as his spirit was descending was, "Hey God, You're making a mistake. I'm going the wrong way!" But He really wasn't. So when you hear Dad tell the story, he says emphatically, "I know for a fact that baptism in water will not save you, because I was baptized in water, and I went to hell."

Dad had this experience three times. But the third time, as he was ascending and coming back up from hell into his body, he began to pray and repent. He asked in the Name of Jesus for the forgiveness of sins that comes only through that Name.

We need to understand that there is *no* other name under Heaven by which we must be saved! But, you see, many people want the easy way out. They want to believe statements, such as: "Join the church, and then you can do anything you want." Or "You're all right, just try to do the right thing in life." But, no, apart from receiving Jesus Christ as Savior, you are *not* "all right." You're spiritually dead in your sins.

The Third Baptism:
The Baptism in the Holy Spirit

Now let's look briefly at the third baptism I mentioned; the baptism in the Holy Spirit with the evidence of speaking in other tongues. A believer can be baptized in the Holy Spirit and speak with other tongues as the Spirit gives him utterance because Jesus said, *"For John truly baptized with water; but ye shall be baptized with the Holy Ghost not many days hence"* (Acts 1:5). Jesus said this just before He ascended on High.

Jesus also declared, "In My Name they shall speak with new tongues" (Mark 16:17). So you see, it's all done in the Name of Jesus! Everything we have in our Christian life is tied up in the Name of Jesus.

Named for Fame

Names were important throughout the Word of God. People's names meant something. In the New Testament, I want you to notice that many times people would address Jesus as "Jesus of Nazareth." Why did they specify "Jesus Christ of Nazareth"? There was a possibility that someone else had that same name, Jesus. But there was only one *Jesus Christ of Nazareth*!

Even today, there's a possibility that within a large group of people, several people in that group could have the same name. So there would have to be some way to further identify those people who shared names in common. Perhaps in Jesus' day, people used the town they were from to identify them, and that was the identifying mark. So when a person identified Jesus as Jesus Christ of Nazareth, he was identifying the one and only Son of God!

The Name of Jesus is the Name that's above every name. It's a Name that we need to realize is backed by deity. Everything that I talked about — salvation, baptism in water, baptism in the Holy Spirit — is backed by that Name. And the way that we change situations and circumstances in life is by using the power of that Name. All I have to do is say, "Jesus." I can sense the anointing begin to build when I repeat that Name!

There's power in that Name! The Name was given to you; you have the authority to use it. Jesus said, "*All* authority, *all* power, has been given to Me both in Heaven and in earth." He has given that Name, with all its power and authority to us who have been born again into the Body of Christ through that Name. Now use that Name to conquer! Use that Name to receive what you need from God's Word! Use that Name so that your joy may be full (John 16:24)! There's power in the **majestic Name of Jesus!**

Chapter 6
The Name in Prayer

In this chapter, I'm going to discuss how to use the Name of Jesus in prayer. Whether you're exercising your spiritual authority in the Name, praying in the Name, or speaking the Name in adoration, there's power in the Name of Jesus!

In John chapter 16, Jesus tells us how to use His Name effectively in prayer.

> **JOHN 16:23,24**
> **23 And in that day ye shall ask me [Jesus] nothing. Verily, verily, I say unto you, Whatsoever ye shall ask the Father IN MY NAME, he will give it you.**
> **24 Hitherto have ye asked nothing in my name: ask, and ye shall receive, that your joy may be full.**

In the literal Greek, these verses read: "And in that day Me, you will not question no thing. Truly, truly I tell you, whatever you ask the Father, He will give you in the Name of Me. Until now, you ask not no thing. In the Name of Me ask and you will receive that the joy of you may be having been filled."

A clearer translation of that interpretation would read, "In that day you will no longer ask Me anything. I tell you the truth, My Father will give you whatever you ask in My Name. Until now, you have not asked for anything in My Name. Ask, and you will receive that your joy will be complete!" (*NIV*).

Notice the phrase in verse 23 "in that day." What day is Jesus talking about? He is talking about the new Day — the time *after* His death, burial, and resurrection when He would ascend back to the Father and bring the New Covenant into effect.

Verse 24 says, *"Hitherto have ye asked nothing in my name: ask, and ye shall receive, that your joy may be full."* The word "hitherto" means *up till now* or *until this present time*.

You see, prior to Jesus' death, burial, and resurrection, He operated on earth as a man anointed by the Holy Ghost. He didn't operate His ministry and perform the miracles that He did as the divine Son of God. The Bible says, *"How God ANOINTED Jesus of Nazareth with the Holy Ghost and with power: who went about doing good, and healing all that were oppressed of the devil. . ."* (Acts 10:38). So when Jesus said, "Hitherto" or "Up till this time," He was talking about the time when He would be crucified, raised from the dead, and ascended to sit at the right hand of the Father.

Now look at John 16:26: *"At that day ye shall ask in my name: and I say not unto you, that I will pray the Father for you.*" This verse is a little blind to us in the *King James Version*. Another translation says, "At that day you shall ask in my name; I will do it for you." Jesus was telling us that we ourselves would be able to pray to the Father — in that powerful Name, the Name of Jesus!

Prayer Truths

There is a real lack of knowledge among many people concerning New Testament prayer. For example, have you ever heard someone ask God for something and conclude the prayer with the phrase "for Jesus' sake"? We aren't to pray *for Jesus' sake*; we are to pray *in Jesus' Name*! We are to conclude our praying to the Father in the Name of Jesus. We can say, ". . . in Jesus' Name, amen," and that's the end of that. In other words, we are to count on whatever we pray about in line with God's Word to come to pass in that Name!

So it's incorrect to conclude our prayers with ". . . for Jesus' sake." Why? Because Jesus doesn't need anything; but *we* do! So we pray for *our* sake, not *His*! The Bible doesn't say, "Ask it for My *sake*." It says, "Ask in My *Name*"!

After Jesus instructed us to ask in His Name, He said, ". . . *ye shall receive, that your joy may be full"* (v. 24)! Yet many people pray to the Father in Jesus' Name and then tack on the phrase ". . . if it be Thy will." But Jesus didn't tell us to pray that kind of prayer when asking God for something. He didn't say to ask the Father in His Name and then add, "If it be Thy will." No, He said, "Ask the Father in My Name, and He *will!"*

There is only one type of praying in which you would pray, "If it be Thy will," and that is the prayer of consecration. In other words, when you pray to God about His will for your life and what direction you should take, it's all right to use the phrase "If it be Thy will."

But there is a balance in some cases when praying about the area of God's will concerning where a person should minister. In other words, every ministry opportunity doesn't always need to be prayed about.

For example, sometimes RHEMA Bible Training Center graduates will complain to me that they don't have anywhere to preach. I always ask them, "Have you received any invitations to preach at all?"

Many of them say, "Well, yes, I did receive an invitation, but I prayed about it and didn't feel like the Lord wanted me to go there."

I always say, "I want to ask you a question: Are you called to preach?"

"Oh, yes. I'm called to preach."

"Then I want to tell you something. If you're
called to preach, and you only have one place to go
preach, I believe I'd get over there and preach!"

That confuses some of them. They say, "Why, I
thought I was supposed to pray about every invitation to see if it was the Lord's will for me to go there
and preach."

So let me share a quick word of wisdom with
anyone reading this book who may have a call to
preach. If you are called to the ministry and someone has given you an invitation to preach, the only
time you need to pray using the phrase "If it be thy
will" is when you have more invitations than you
have days available in which to minister! Until that
time comes, you'd better just start going out and
ministering where the door opens!

Back to prayer now. We know that when it
comes to asking God for something in His Word, we
don't have to ask Him what His will is. Because
*God has already explicitly stated His will in His
Word!* God is Supreme, and He has fully laid down
His will in His holy written Word. And when we
understand what God's will is, we can ask Him in
prayer in the Name of Jesus and know with confidence that we've received what we asked for
(1 John 5:14).

Understanding the Name of Jesus and the power that's in the Name *will* cause you to be a success in every area of life. But did you know that sometimes others, even fellow Christians, will have a problem with your using the Name of Jesus, especially when they see the results? Some don't seem to mind so much while you're believing God for something in Jesus' Name. But when the answer comes, suddenly they have a problem with that!

I have actually seen officials of some denominational organizations get upset because one of their ministers was being blessed financially as a result of his exercising authority in the Name of Jesus.

Well, I thank God for those organizations. I love the people in those organizations, but when it comes to choosing between obeying God or man, we need to obey God! I want to receive the best that God has for me! How about you?

Boundaries to Your Spiritual Authority

Also, we need to understand when it comes to asking God to meet our needs, we have the authority of the Name of Jesus. But that authority doesn't extend to someone else's life. In other words, you can't push your authority off on others. Their wills are involved.

You don't have authority to use the Name to get something for someone else unless he is a baby Christian. And you *never* have the authority to push something off on someone against his will.

So many times we want to pray for others in the Name of Jesus, but their thinking and their believing can nullify our faith. They have a right to believe the way they want to believe. God made us all free moral agents to choose how we want to choose.

I have a few old college friends who don't agree with me on certain subjects. They don't understand what it means to believe God for healing or finances or praying to God in Jesus' Name, expecting to receive an answer. These people are saved and filled with the Spirit. Some of them are in the ministry. Yet we don't agree on certain subjects.

You see, a person can be saved, filled with the Spirit, and live right in line with the Word in some areas and yet not live in line with the Word in other areas, such as receiving his needs met.

There's no need arguing with people you don't agree with. I refuse to get into an arguing match with others who don't agree with me. Some of my friends who don't believe like I do in every area will ask me to preach for them. And if they ask me to preach on a certain subject and avoid other subjects, I will do just that.

"But, Rev. Hagin," you ask, "don't you think you'd be compromising your stand?"

No, I don't. When you go into another pastor's church and preach for him, *he* has the authority in that church, not you. So as a visitor, you are to come under subjection to the authority that he is entrusted with in that church. But you can always preach "Christ and Him crucified" (1 Cor. 1:23,24; 2:2)! I don't have to preach on the baptism in the Holy Ghost, healing, finances, and so forth. I can just preach Christ as Savior, because if that pastor is a Christian, then he believes in Christ the Savior, crucified and risen!

I enjoy fellowship with people who don't have the Holy Spirit and who don't believe in speaking in tongues, healing, or prosperity. As long as they believe in being saved by the blood of the Lord Jesus Christ and living in line with that, I can fellowship with them!

Now that doesn't mean I want to be close friends with them. I want to closely associate with those of like-precious faith. But there's a difference in fellowshipping with someone and being close friends with him.

So we know that we can't use our God-given authority in the Name of Jesus to get something for someone else unless he or she wants it. In other words, we can't pray for something for someone else against his or her will.

But on the other hand, the unbelief of someone else can't nullify your praying in Jesus' Name for things concerning your own life. The unbelief of others can't hinder your receiving what belongs to you in that Name!

Some people have some strange beliefs about what Jesus taught on prayer. Some when they pray, have the mentality, *Maybe God will do it, and maybe He won't*. But Jesus didn't say in John 16:23 and 24, "Up until now, you have asked nothing in My Name. Ask; however, sometimes I may say, 'Yes,' sometimes I may say, 'No,' and sometimes I may say, 'Wait awhile.'"

I've actually heard that taught! But that's not what Jesus said. He said, "Ask, and you *shall* receive" (v. 24). Now Jesus didn't put a time limit here. He simply said, "Ask, and you shall receive." He didn't say, "You shall receive by six o'clock tomorrow." Sometimes I think we mess things up ourselves and hurt our own faith by trying to put God on our timetable.

God will answer you when you pray according to his Word and continue to believe His Word without wavering. It may not happen tomorrow, the next day, or even the next week or month, but it will happen if you do your part. There have been things I've prayed for that took six to eight months to receive, but I received them because I believed that God would do what He said He would do!

Someone said, "Well, I just don't know about all that walking by faith business. I want my answer now or not at all." Sometimes I think we get too hung up on the timing of things, rather than just learning to count it done when we pray and to praise God in faith until the answer comes. Instead of getting hung up on what we see or don't see and relying on our senses, let's get hung up on the fact that there's power in the Name! And Jesus said we could use that Name in prayer.

The Name of Jesus is a Name that we need to learn to appreciate. And as we learn more about the power that's in the Name, I believe we will appreciate the Name more and more. The Name of Jesus needs to be a reality in every part of our life. That Name should be in our thoughts, our prayers, our witnessing, in our preaching, and in our living.

Yet so many Christians don't understand what they have in the Name of Jesus. Many understand how to use the Name of Jesus in prayer, because they've been taught to conclude their prayers "in Jesus' Name." But not as many really understand the significance of the Name.

As I said, because some people have been taught a certain way, they just repeat the Name of Jesus in prayer in a sort of parrot-like fashion. Have you ever heard a parrot talk? The parrot only repeats what it's been taught. Sad to say, some people are just like parrots when they speak the Name of Jesus since they only say it because someone told them to or because they heard someone else speaking it.

But it doesn't work that way. Most of the time when people just repeat the Name of Jesus in prayer, they don't even expect it to work. Sometimes, people will ask me to agree with them in prayer using Matthew 18:19 and 20. I'll agree with their prayer, or I'll pray in the Name of Jesus. Then I'll say, "Do you agree with that prayer?"

"Oh, yes. I agree!"

"Well, is it done?" I'll ask.

"Yes, yes! It's done! It's done!"

Sometimes I'll see some of those same people later. So I'll check up on the situation, trying to get a testimony out of them. And some of them say, "Well, it didn't happen. But I didn't much expect it to, anyway." Yet when I prayed with them, they said they agreed!

Do you know what those people did? They just *mentally* agreed — they agreed with their mind, not with their heart. They said they agreed, because they knew they were *expected* to agree. But they only did it because it was expected of them, and their heart wasn't in it.

Many times when I'm counseling people or when people ask me for advice, I begin by asking them some questions so I can "locate" them spiritually to find out where they are in their faith walk. I say to them, "I want you to answer me honestly, so please don't tell me what you think I want to hear. Don't say what you think you're supposed to say or what you think you're expected to say." You see, the only way I can help someone is if he tells me what he or she *really* believes.

Those people who asked me to pray and agree with them quoted the right scripture and talked the right talk. They even repeated the Name of Jesus. Yet it didn't work; nothing happened. Why? Because they were talking from their head and not from their heart. The Bible says that it's *". . . with the HEART man believeth unto righteousness; and with the mouth confession is made unto salvation"* (Rom. 10:10).

You see, your heart is your spirit. Those people were *mentally* involved, but they weren't *spiritually* involved. It's possible to repeat scriptures and make confessions out of your head and not your heart, simply because you have been taught to make those confessions. That's why meditation in the Word is so important. The Word of God has to be in your heart for it to be effective. The Psalmist said, *"Thy word have I hid in mine HEART, that I might not sin against thee"* (Ps. 119:11).

So if you're going to get the Word to work for you, it's got to come from your heart, not your head. If it's just coming from your head, it's only mental agreement, not faith. But if it's coming from your heart, your heart or spirit can bring the natural man — the soul and body — into submission to your spirit, to what you're believing with your spirit. *Because believing begins in the heart.*

You know, if people really understood and believed what the Word of God says, they'd get more excited about it. When the Word is real to you, you can't help but get excited about God's "exceeding great and precious promises" (2 Peter 1:4)!

When you believe the Word of God with your heart, you're actually believing it in the power of the Name of Jesus, and you will stay with it, come what may. Sink or swim, go over or go under, nothing will move or distract you — because you know you have the answer! You've got the answer even before you see it come to pass, because you've got the Word in your spirit, not just in your head. You're hooked on it! And when you stick with God and His Word, God will stick with you!

Many people say they aren't receiving from God or that they feel as if God has left them. But the only reason they feel like God has left them is, they left God and His Word first! They didn't stay with the Word, so God had nothing to make good in their life. He doesn't leave them, but He won't perform His Word where His Word isn't welcome. God is a gentleman.

In the natural, a gentleman won't stick around where he's not welcome. I know if I was at someone's house and found out he didn't want me there, I wouldn't be able to get out the door fast enough! I don't want to be somewhere I'm not welcome.

Now just because a person isn't honoring God's Word and standing on it in faith doesn't mean God, Jesus, or the Holy Spirit will leave that person. The Holy Spirit will continue to try to woo and teach him and try to get him to walk in the light of the Word. He will try to deal with the person.

So don't misunderstand me. If you're not sticking with the Word, believing it in your heart and confessing it, God won't leave you. He just won't be able to get involved in the situations and circumstances of your life like He wants to, because you are not cooperating with Him.

'In That Day'

Now let's look again briefly at Jesus' statement that I opened this chapter with involving "that day" in which we would use His Name in prayer. When did Jesus' Name become available to use in prayer to the Father? The answer can be found once again in the classic promise Jesus made regarding the use of His Name in prayer, in John 16.

> **JOHN 16:23,24**
> **23 And in that day ye shall ask me nothing. Verily, verily, I say unto you, Whatsoever ye shall ask the Father in my name, he will give it you.**
> **24 Hitherto have ye asked nothing in my name: ask, and ye shall receive, that your joy may be full.**

Look at the phrase "in that day" in verse 23: *"And IN THAT DAY ye shall ask me nothing. Verily, verily, I say unto you, Whatsoever ye shall ask the Father in my name, he will give it you."* What day was Jesus talking about? Monday? Tuesday? Last Thursday? Saturday before last?

My dad and I used to horse around and "roughhouse" for fun when I was a kid. He'd say, "I'm going to knock you into the middle of next week!" I'd always say, "Go ahead; I'll just be ahead of you!" Of course, we were only kidding one another, but I said that to illustrate the fact that we automatically think in terms of time — seconds, minutes, hours, days, weeks, and so forth.

But Jesus wasn't referring to a particular day of the week when He said, *". . . IN THAT DAY ye shall ask me nothing. Verily, verily, I say unto you, Whatsoever ye shall ask the Father in my name, he will give it you."* He was talking about the day, era, or age after Calvary — the day of the New Covenant — including the day in which you and I live today.

Jesus made that promise just before He went to Calvary. We could quote that scripture like this: "In that day, the day of the New Covenant, you shall ask Me nothing. But whatever you ask the Father in My Name, He will give it."

Then John 16:24 says, *"Hitherto have ye asked nothing in my name . . . ."* In other words, Jesus was saying, "Up until now — up until this day — you have asked nothing in My Name . . . ." Because the disciples had never asked anything in His Name before. They hadn't used that Name in prayer.

The rest of John 16:24 says, *". . . ask, and ye shall receive, that your joy may be full."* The Book of James says, *". . . ye have not, because ye ask not"* (v. 4:2). So God is telling us to *ask* today that our joy may be full! But many people simply don't ask. They don't understand their rights to go straight to the Father in Jesus' Name.

We Have Not Because We Ask Not!

Have you ever been on a special committee in your school or church that had to plan a party or some kind of gathering? If so, there were probably times you needed something, such as a formal approval, money, or the use of certain resources and supplies. You've no doubt heard or used this phrase, "Well, it won't hurt to *ask*. All they can do is say no."

I want you to understand that as a believer, you don't have to form a committee, do a lot of planning, and wonder whether or not you should ask God for what you need! God said to *ask*! And after we ask, we don't have to "wait and see" if He's going to say yes or no! Because Jesus already said, ". . . *ask* [in My Name], *and ye shall receive, that your joy may be full*" (John 16:24).

Now who is supposed to ask? *The person who wants something!*

Too many times people go to others trying to get *them* to ask God on their behalf. For example, if you had brothers or sisters when you were growing up, did you ever send one of them in to ask Mom or Dad for something on your behalf? Maybe you thought that one of them was on better terms with your parents, and that they didn't necessarily want what they were asking for. But *you* wanted it, so you sent one of them in to ask for it. You figured your brother or sister might get a "yes" answer, and that you would get a "no."

But, you see, that's not the way it works in the Kingdom of God. Jesus said *we* are supposed to do the asking! We're supposed to use the Name in prayer and receive answers — that our joy may be full!

Chapter 7
All in the Name

We know that as believers, we possess the Name of Jesus and the right to use that Name in life. Maybe we haven't exercised our authority in that Name as we should have. If that is so, we need to correct this and begin to believe in the power in the Name of Jesus. Because every good thing that God has given to us, He's given through that Name.

COLOSSIANS 3:17
17 And whatsoever ye do in word or deed, do all IN THE NAME OF THE LORD JESUS, giving thanks to God and the Father by him.

The believers in the Early Church were taught this important truth of doing everything in the Name of Jesus. So they must have understood the benefits in the Name of Jesus better than believers seem to today. They probably used and appropriated the Name continually in every area of their lives. Just as the Name should be a part of our everyday lives, too, because the Scripture says, ". . . *whatsoever ye do in word or deed, do all in the name of the Lord Jesus . . . .*"

The Early Church lived with the Name of Jesus on their lips. Everywhere they went, they were conscious of Jesus. And it produced results, not only in their lives, but in those who were outside the Church — sinners.

Those outside of the Church feared the Name of Jesus. For instance, when Peter and John were taken into custody after the man was healed at the Gate called Beautiful, the priests and the religious people said, *"But that it spread no further among the people, let us straitly threaten them, that they speak henceforth to no man in this name"* (Acts 4:17). Then verse 18 says, *"And they called them, and commanded them not to speak at all nor teach in the name of Jesus."*

So the Name of Jesus should be on our lips at all times. When you understand the magnitude of that Name and are continually conscious of it, others will notice. Verse 3 of Acts 4 says, *". . . when they saw the boldness of Peter and John, and perceived that they were unlearned and ignorant men, they marvelled; and THEY TOOK KNOWLEDGE OF THEM, that they had been with Jesus."*

Notice this verse didn't say, "They took knowledge of them that they'd been *in a prayer meeting.*" Or "They took knowledge of them that they had been *on a long fast.*" No, the people noticed that they had been *with Jesus*!

Do All in the Name

Do *you* want to get noticed? Start walking with Jesus! Start doing everything you do in His Name. Should the Church in the first century be different from the Church today? No, we're the same Church with the same Holy Spirit, and the same power. The Name of Jesus belongs to us today just as it belonged to the Church of the Colossians — those to whom Paul wrote, ". . . *whatsoever ye do in word or deed, do all in the name of the Lord Jesus . . .*" (Col. 3:17).

That same exhortation applies to the Church today, wherever we are, because there is only one Church of the Lord Jesus Christ. So we should continually be growing in our understanding of that Name so we can live every moment of every day in the Name of Jesus!

Writing to the Church at Colosse, the Apostle Paul gave the instructions: "Whatever you do in word or deed, do it in the Name of Jesus." In other words, if you sweep the floor, sweep it in the Name of Jesus. If you mow the lawn, do it in the Name of

Jesus. If you teach school, teach in the Name of Jesus. If you're a singer, sing in the Name of Jesus.

Whatever we do, we are to *do* it in the Name. We are to *live* in the Name of Jesus!

Lifting Up Jesus Brings the Anointing

When I was a kid, I used to go with my dad to conventions and meetings. Once when we went to a convention, someone got up on the platform to sing a special. The person sang "perfectly" — all the words were enunciated clearly and the hand gestures were just right. When the person finished, everyone said, "Oh, praise the Lord, that was good."

Then after that person sang, a couple came to the platform to sing another special. They didn't even go to the center of the stage, they just stood on the side of the platform. The man had an old guitar that looked like it was bought at a second-hand store. And he didn't play it; he "beat" on it!

He began to beat on that thing, and they started singing something that sounded sort of off-key. But I want to tell you, they sang from the bottom of their hearts and lifted up Jesus. And by the time they finished singing, everyone in the place was shouting and praising the Lord!

I recalled the incident many years later and asked Dad about it. I asked him why one singer who was so professional evoked so little response from the congregation. And why the other singers who weren't nearly as talented "brought the house down" with the power of God.

Dad said, "Well, the one singer got up in his own might and in his own strength. But that couple got up there singing unto Jesus."

In other words, they weren't trying to bring glory to themselves or trying to get any meetings for themselves. They were just glorifying Jesus!

You see, Colossians 3:17 says, ". . . *whatsoever ye do in word or deed, do all in the name of the Lord Jesus, giving thanks to God and the Father by him.*"

When someone does something in the Name of Jesus — as unto the Lord — the anointing "splashes," as it were, over on everyone else around him. And everyone is blessed!

That happens many times in prayer meetings. People could be praying all over a room, but there might be a certain group that seems to really be "going after it" in the Spirit. If you'll go over to where they are and begin praying near that group, the power of God will get on you, and you'll get blessed!

Whatever you do in life, if you will do it in the Name of Jesus, you will be blessed, your work will be blessed, and others will be blessed too! It's all in the Name!

Colossians 3:17 goes right along with Acts 17:28: *"For in him we live, and move, and have our being . . . ."* Many people want to apply Acts 17:28 only spiritually. But you take the spiritual with you everywhere you go in the natural. You live in Him; you move in Him; and you have your being in Him — it's all in the Name of Jesus!

The Name of Jesus Brings Peace And Lifts Up Your Spirit

Since the Lord began dealing with me along these lines, I've been extremely careful to do all in the Name of Jesus. For example, if someone starts giving me a bunch of negative reports about something, I whisper to myself, "In the Name of Jesus. In the Name of Jesus."

Thank God for the Word and for the power of good, Word-based confessions. But I have found out that when you start feeling down, you can just start saying, "In the Name of Jesus." And you can't say that Name very long without experiencing God's peace and being lifted up in your spirit!

So I encourage you to say that Name out loud: "Jesus!" Get somewhere by yourself and scream it out if you have to! That Name will change the atmosphere. The devil can't stay around where you're using the Name properly.

That verse, ". . . *whatsoever ye do in word or deed, do all in the name of the Lord Jesus, giving thanks to God and the Father by him*" is talking about "whatsoever ye do" every day, every minute, every hour! Do all in the Name of the Lord Jesus! You can even go to sleep in the Name of Jesus. Just say, "I'm going to lie down and go to sleep, and I'm going to sleep peacefully in the Name of Jesus." Then when you get up, do so in the Name of Jesus, saying, "This is the day that You have made. I will rejoice and be glad in it!"

So, we know that we should do everything, whether in word or deed, in the Name of Jesus. As I said, we are to *live* in that Name!

We Are To Live Holy in the Name

First Corinthians 6:11 says, *"And such were some of you: but ye are washed, but ye are sanctified, but ye are justified in the name of the Lord Jesus, and by the Spirit of our God."*

The *New International Version* says it this way:

> **1 CORINTHIANS 6:11 (*NIV*)**
> 11 And that is what some of you were. But you were
> washed, you were sanctified, you were justified in
> the name of the Lord Jesus Christ and by the Spirit
> of our God.

Let's read that passage in its context, so we can understand the phrase "And that is what some of you were."

> **1 CORINTHIANS 6:9-11 (*NIV*)**
> 9   Do you not know that the wicked will not
> inherit the kingdom of God? Do not be deceived:
> Neither the sexually immoral nor idolaters nor
> adulterers nor male prostitutes nor homosexual
> offenders
> 10 nor thieves nor the greedy nor drunkards nor
> slanderers nor swindlers will inherit the kingdom
> of God.
> 11 AND THAT IS WHAT SOME OF YOU WERE. But
> you were washed . . . sanctified . . . justified IN THE
> NAME OF THE LORD JESUS CHRIST . . . .

It is very clear from reading this that people in certain categories, unless they accept the Lord Jesus Christ and are delivered, are not going to see Heaven. It doesn't matter whether they go to church or even say they're preachers — apart from the Name of the Lord Jesus Christ, no one will "inherit the Kingdom of God."

Someone might say, "Well, I have my rights. I can do whatever I want to do." Yes, you have rights as a human being to make your own choices. But God says that certain things are wrong to do. And if you do them, spiritually, you are wrong. According to God, you need to repent.

Now I'm not saying that God doesn't love such people who practice wrongdoing. Jesus loves them; He died for them. As a matter of fact, He died for the sins of the whole world. That's why it says, *"Neither is there salvation in any other: for there is none other name under heaven given among men, whereby we must be saved"* (Acts 4:12).

We as Christians should want to help those bound with sin and to lead them to Jesus the Savior. But we can't help anyone by siding in with his wrongdoing.

You see, where morals are involved, the Bible is plain on the subject. We have no leeway. The Bible is very explicit on the subject of sin, such as sexual immorality. Then First Corinthians 6 goes on to talk about thieves, extortioners (greedy people who will try to get money from someone else any way they can) drunkards, and slanderers (1 Cor. 6:10).

Do you know what a slanderer is? A slanderer is someone who talks badly about other people.

You'll see this sin of slander in the Church many times. Christians fall into this trap of talking badly about someone or even repeating what they heard someone else say. There are some who say they're Christians that need to get delivered from a wagging tongue! They fall under the category of slanderers. Every time you're around some of these people, they have something to tell you about someone else. "Have you heard the latest?" they'll say.

I cringe on the inside when I hear someone say, "Have you heard the latest?" and then proceed to talk about things they have no business talking about. I always try to change the subject so I don't have to listen to them. I'm just not interested in hearing it. Most of the time, the stories are only about fifty-percent correct. The rest is speculation, but some people tell it as if it were truth.

It's slander when you talk against someone's name. I get especially upset when people talk about something someone did as if whatever they did just happened yesterday — then come to find out, it happened *years* ago. The person they're slandering has long since repented. He was forgiven and has gone on with God. But other Christians — some of his own brothers and sisters in Christ — are still holding him accountable in unforgiveness, slandering his name!

We'd better be careful how we talk about others.
Even if we hear something about someone that's
true, we need to be careful not to repeat it to others.
The Bible says that if you see someone who is overtaken in a sin or has done wrong, you should *restore*
him, not *talk about* him.

GALATIANS 6:1
1 Brethren, if a man be overtaken in a fault, ye
which are spiritual, restore such an one in the
spirit of meekness; considering thyself, lest thou
also be tempted.

First Corinthians 6:10 also lists swindlers among
those who practice wrongdoing. People who are "fast
talkers" in business and cheat other people are
swindlers. Swindlers say one thing, and then do
another. They are dishonest. And anyone who does
it knows nothing about Jesus' Name.

First Corinthians 6:9 and 10 lists a terrible "catalog" of sin.

1 CORINTHIANS 6:9,10
9 Know ye not that the unrighteous shall not
inherit the kingdom of God? Be not deceived: neither
fornicators, nor idolaters, nor adulterers, nor effemi-
nate, nor abusers of themselves with mankind,
10 Nor thieves, nor covetous, nor drunkard, nor
revilers, nor extortioners, shall inherit the kingdom
of God.

But, praise God, there's power in the Name of Jesus!

1 CORINTHIANS 6:11
11 And such were some of you: but ye are WASHED, but ye are SANCTIFIED, but ye are JUSTIFIED in the NAME OF THE LORD JESUS, and by the Spirit of our God.

The power that's in the Name of Jesus can deliver a person from all the things mentioned in First Corinthians 6:9 and 10. Maybe you've already experienced the cleansing, sanctifying, justifying power in the Name of Jesus! Others still need to experience that power in their lives.

So we know there's deliverance and forgiveness in the Name of Jesus.

We Are To Give Thanks in the Name

Not only do we receive blessings and benefits in that Name, we are to give *thanks* in the Name.

Many Christians give thanks to God, all right. But there is a secret to giving thanks *in the Name*.

Ephesians 5:20 says, *"Giving thanks ALWAYS for all things unto God and the Father in the name of our Lord Jesus Christ."* Hebrews 13:15 goes right along with this verse in Ephesians concerning how often we should give thanks in the Name.

Hebrews 13 says something else about thanksgiving in connection with the Name.

> **HEBREWS 13:15 (*NIV*)**
> **15 Through Jesus, therefore, let us *continually* offer to God a sacrifice of praise — the fruit of lips that confess his name.**

That word "continually" means *all the time*! Now that doesn't mean that twenty-four hours a day we should continuously praise God with our mouths! But we *should* continually — twenty-four hours a day — have a thankful *attitude* toward God.

You know, when I'm driving my car, I find myself whispering over and over, "Thank You, Jesus. Thank You, Jesus. Thank You, Jesus." My wife will sometimes ask me, "Is something the matter?" I'll say, "No, I'm just thanking the Lord." We need to *continually* thank the Lord!

We just don't do enough thanking. I think so many of our problems would be solved in life if we would continually offer up the sacrifice of praise from our lips, giving thanks to His Name.

We Are To Anoint the Sick in the Name

James 5:14 says, *"Is any sick among you? let him call for the elders of the church; and let them pray over him, ANOINTING HIM with oil IN THE NAME OF THE LORD."*

As I said before, it seems as if everything the early believers did, they did in the Name of Jesus. And since the *early* believers did all these things in the Name of Jesus — the *latter* believers need to do them in the Name of Jesus too!

In James 5:14, we learn that believers are to pray for and anoint the sick in the Name of Jesus. Verse 15 shows us the result of that kind of praying and anointing in the Name.

> **JAMES 5:15**
> **15 And the prayer of faith shall save the sick, and the Lord shall raise him up; and if he have committed sins, they shall be forgiven him.**

The Bible teaches that we are to live holy, give thanks, and pray for the sick — all in the Name of Jesus! But, more importantly, we are to *believe* on the Lord Jesus Christ and His Name. In fact, before you can do all these other things I've discussed, you first have to believe on the Name. Actually, First John 3:23 says it's a *commandment*. So we are commanded to believe on the Name of Jesus and to love one another.

> **1 JOHN 3:23**
> **23 And this is his commandment, That we should believe on the name of his Son Jesus Christ, and love one another, as he gave us commandment.**

There's power in keeping God's command to love one another. And we know that there's power in the Name of Jesus. So in keeping God's command to believe on the Name and to walk in love, there is great power!

We Are To Exercise
Spiritual Authority in the Name

It is true that we have power and authority in the Name of Jesus, but we must learn to *exercise* that authority before we will see any results or benefits.

Mark 16 lists the signs that will follow the preaching of the Word and the use of the Name.

MARK 16:17-19
17 ... these signs shall follow them that believe; In my name shall they cast out devils; they shall speak with new tongues;
18 They shall take up serpents; and if they drink any deadly thing, it shall not hurt them; they shall lay hands on the sick, and they shall recover.
19 So then after the Lord had spoken unto them, he was received up into heaven, and sat on the right hand of God.

I want you to notice the first sign in this passage that Jesus said would follow or accompany believing ones in His name. "... *In my Name shall they CAST OUT DEVILS . . ."* (v. 17). Jesus said the first sign that would accompany His believing ones was casting out demons. In other words, we can exercise authority over demon power in the Name of Jesus. This verse doesn't say, "These signs shall follow only *preachers*." No, it says, "These signs shall follow them that *believe*."

Are you a believer? Then you have authority and power in the Name of Jesus!

The Word of God is our "textbook" to guide and instruct us. So let's look at a passage in Acts 16 that goes into detail about our spiritual authority in the Name.

> **ACTS 16:16-18 (*NIV*)**
> **16 Once when we were going to the place of prayer, we were met by a slave girl who had a spirit by which she predicted the future. She earned a great deal of money for her owners by fortune-telling.**
> **17 This girl followed Paul and the rest of us, shouting, "These men are servants of the Most High God, who are telling you the way to be saved."**
> **18 She kept this up for many days . . . .**

Now this girl who was shouting the "praises" of Paul and Silas was telling the truth! Yet her lifestyle wasn't exactly good advertising, because she had an evil spirit.

This girl followed Paul and Silas for many days, and during that time, Paul had put up with her shouting. But then look at the rest of verse 18.

ACTS 16:18 (NIV)
18 . . . Finally Paul became so troubled that he
turned round and said to the spirit, "In the name of
Jesus Christ I command you to come out of her!" At
that moment the spirit left her.

This "slave girl" or "damsel," as the *King James
Version* puts it, had earned a great deal of money
for her owners through fortune-telling. We need to
understand today that we are not to mess around
with horoscopes, psychics, and so forth. In our day,
we would call this fortune-teller a psychic. "Psychic" is just a modern word for fortune-teller. You
see, the devil keeps trying to dress up his product!

Acts chapter 16 says the girl had a spirit by
which she predicted the future. But no matter what
it's called, it's still the same thing, and the Bible
forbids our association with those kinds of practices
(Deut. 18:14). Participating in those activities will
mislead and take you away from the truth.

I want you to notice that when Paul spoke, he
didn't speak to the girl, but to the spirit. The Bible
says that we don't wrestle against flesh and blood
". . . *but against principalities, against powers,
against the rulers of the darkness of this world,
against spiritual wickedness in high places*" (Eph.
6:12).

In other words, people aren't our problem; it's
the evil spirits that *influence* people that are the
real problem.

Paul said to that spirit, ". . . *I command thee IN THE NAME OF JESUS CHRIST to come out of her . . .*" (Acts 16:18). And that spirit came out of her!

You see, many people try to deal with the devil by praying in tongues. But you don't deal with the devil by praying in tongues. The Bible specifically says that if you're going to cast out the devil, you do it by the Name of Jesus! That's where the power and the authority is — in the Name!

We simply need to understand that the Name is still the same Name today in the "Latter Church" as it was in the Early Church. And that the Name of Jesus still has the same power over evil spirits as it did back then.

Many people who don't understand the operation of demons try to deal with the *person* when an evil spirit is manifesting itself through someone. But again, it's not the individual we are to deal with; it's the spirit controlling the individual that we must deal with.

Now when we in America talk about a person being demon-possessed, most of the time, we're not talking about true demon-possession. People who are really demon-possessed are stark-raving mad! Most of the time, what people think of as a demon-possessed person is someone who may be *oppressed*, *obsessed*, or *influenced* by a demon or evil spirit. In other words, he might be *yielding* to an evil spirit, but that doesn't mean that he is *possessed* by an evil spirit.[1]

You probably don't know what demon possession is unless you've visited some foreign fields and witnessed true demon-possession firsthand. If you have, you understand from experience the difference between someone who is actually possessed, and someone who is just being influenced by an evil spirit.

A person can yield to an evil spirit without being possessed and taken over by an evil spirit. For instance, a person could yield himself to an evil spirit and carry on and say and do things under the influence of that spirit. The person is not possessed; he's just yielding to an evil spirit. He might seem rational one minute, but the next minute, he's acting irrational because he's yielded to an evil spirit.

Many Christians have neglected the use of the Name of Jesus in dealing with demon power, because they've not understood the power that's in the Name or how to use their spiritual authority in that Name.

Excess and Error
In Dealing With Demon Power

The devil has done a good job getting people off-track when it comes to dealing with demon power.

One way he's done this is by deceiving them into thinking they have to put people in a chair and scream at them in tongues to get an evil spirit to leave!

Some Christians actually believe that. They think that in order to get an evil spirit to leave a person, they have to put the person in a chair and pray in tongues in his or her face for hours, screaming, yelling, and trying to have conversations with the devil. But while they're doing that, the devil doesn't have to do anything! He doesn't have to respond, because they're not using their God-given authority in the Name of Jesus. All they are doing is having a "shouting-match" with the devil!

But when you use the Name of Jesus, something happens! There's power in that Name!

Don't Neglect the Holy Spirit's Leading

I want to share with you an illustration that shows the power of the Name of Jesus and the benefit of yielding to the Holy Spirit!

In 1958, I was working at an auto parts store in Garland, Texas, and Dad called me one day from St. Louis where he was ministering. "The Lord said for you to come up here," he said.

So I said, "Well, I'd like to work about three more weeks before I have to quit and go back to college."

But Dad said, "No, I was praying last night, and the Lord said to tell you to get up here."

So I went to St. Louis, and while I was gone, a string of robberies took place in Garland. We eventually found out that there was a guy from out-of-town with a car just like mine who was robbing people.

Now the local police came to our house because they knew what kind of car I drove. My mom told them, "Why, Ken hasn't been in town for a week!"

So the Holy Spirit knows how to protect people! He told my dad to have me go to St. Louis, and I'm glad I listened to my dad and obeyed him. If I hadn't, it would have been harder to prove my whereabouts during that string of robberies. But, thank God, the robber was caught, and I was spared a whole lot of trouble!

Now I want to relate something that happened while was I in St. Louis with Dad. He was holding a series of meetings. And one morning, someone brought a lady to church and had her sit down in the back of the auditorium, because she was carrying on and making all kinds of noise.

Someone was sitting next to her who was laying hands on this lady and praying in tongues. But that didn't faze the lady one bit! She kept making crazy noises throughout the service.

After the service, Dad said, "We've got to minister to this lady; she has an evil spirit." He asked almost everyone to leave the room, because he didn't want a big crowd of people in there who didn't understand how to deal with the devil. Then Dad grabbed this lady's hands and looked her straight in the eyes. He never prayed in tongues. He just said, "In the Name of Jesus Christ of Nazareth, come out!"

The evil spirit answered, "I don't want to!"

"I know you don't," Dad responded, "but in the Name of Jesus, you'll have to come out!"

At that moment, the woman fell to the floor, writhing, but within minutes, she was completely restored!

You Can't Use the Name
To Violate Another's Will

Back in the early 1970's when I was Dad's crusade director, we were in New York holding a meeting, and I witnessed a similar experience along this line.

After I'd made the announcements, I left the auditorium to go to our book table. As I was walking down the hall toward the book table, I saw some ushers "escorting" a woman toward the door.

As I got closer, I could hear her using every kind of foul language you could think of and some you *couldn't* think of! I said to the ushers, "Leave her alone." Then I began to talk to her, and she settled down a little bit. I told her, "If you want to stay in the service, you may."

She wanted to return to the service, so I had one of our associates keep an eye on her in case she tried to disrupt the service again. I instructed him, "Keep an eye on her and continue to repeat these words: 'In the Name of Jesus.'" I knew that those evil spirits which were influencing her would try to act up again.

My associate sat nearby on one side of this woman, and I sat nearby on the other. Both my associate and I kept repeating "In the Name of Jesus." The woman kept looking back and forth at us, but never said a word. Finally, she got up and started walking up the aisle to the front of the church. She'd seen a seat up front in the middle section right in front of where Dad was standing as he taught.

My associate looked at me, as if to ask me what we should do. I told him, "We'll let it go. Dad's got her now."

I never will forget what happened. Dad was walking along the platform teaching, and this woman started acting up again. So he simply said, "In the Name of Jesus" and kept right on going with his message. About twenty minutes later, she started up again. This time, Dad said, "I *told you* in the Name of Jesus to behave."

And do you know what? She settled down and never did disrupt the service again. After the service, some of the ushers brought the woman to us, and we began talking with her some more. Dad told her, "You can be delivered from that if you want to be."

But she replied, "No, I like it this way. I get attention yielding to this 'thing' that comes upon me."

You know, we couldn't help her. No one could help her as long as she didn't want to be helped.

If someone wants to keep on yielding to an evil spirit, you can't help him. However, in the Name of Jesus, the person does have to be quiet while you're preaching. Because when you're preaching, you have a certain authority to stop any evil spirit that tries to hinder, embarrass, or intimidate you in any way.

That Name belongs to all of us, but we each have to individually use it to take authority in our own lives. We can't use the Name to take authority over someone else's life. But over matters that concern us, we do have authority.

The devil is frightened of Jesus' Name! We need to understand that fact! We need to exercise our authority over the devil when he tries to come against us as we're doing God's will. If we don't use our God-given authority in our own lives, no one else will. Because no one else has authority over the devil in matters that concern us, whether it be our physical health, finances, family, job, or ministry.

Perimeters of Authority

For example, in his own church, a pastor has authority over the enemy in the affairs of that church. The pastor has been set in that church as the leader, the overseer, of that local church and congregation. He also has authority in his own home. But he doesn't have authority over *your* home if you're a member of that church. No, the responsibility of taking authority is *yours* in your own home so that the enemy can't come in to try to steal, kill, and destroy (John 10:10).

A pastor's authority doesn't reach into another pastor's church, either. But he does have a right to exercise authority over the enemy where his own church is concerned.

By way of illustration, there was a certain pastor who was having trouble preaching in his own church. There were good people in that church, but it was hard to preach there. My dad preached in that church and said it was the hardest place to preach he'd ever seen.

So this pastor began to pray and fast about the situation. Then one day he was in the church auditorium just lying on his back, praying and seeking the Lord, when the Lord showed him what the problem was.

He was lying three or four feet behind the pulpit when he began to operate in the gift of discerning of spirits (1 Cor. 12:10). That is a gift of the Holy Spirit by which God lets a person see into the spirit realm.

When the discerning of spirits began to operate, the ceiling of the church just "disappeared," and sitting up in the rafters was what looked like a big baboon! It was an evil spirit that was hindering the preaching of the Word in that church.

The pastor simply said to the spirit, "In the Name of Jesus, you've got to go."

The evil spirit sort of fell down out of the rafters and took a few steps off the platform before stopping. So the pastor said, "You've got to go." But the baboon-like spirit did nothing. Then the pastor said, "In the Name of Jesus, I said you have to go!" The evil spirit took several more steps before stopping to look back at the pastor. The spirit looked pitiful — as if it were pleading with the pastor to let it stay.

"Go!" the pastor said. The evil spirit did nothing. Then the pastor said, "In the Name of Jesus, go!" And the spirit walked out the church door, lingering in front of the church. Then the pastor said, "In the Name of Jesus, get off this property and don't come back on these premises!"

The spirit ran off the premises and down the street about half a block into an old nightclub. That nightclub burned to the ground the following night.

After all of that, the man's church became an *easy* place to preach! Why? Because the pastor used his authority in the Name! I'm not saying that an evil spirit is the problem in every church in which it is hard to preach. But that was the case there.

The pastor shared what happened with a few preachers. He didn't tell it to a whole lot of people, because many don't understand spiritual things. He never did tell the congregation. But after he commanded the spirit to leave, they continually told the pastor, "Your preaching is so much better!" The pastor would just say, "Well, the Spirit of God is moving in our midst."

Stand Your Ground in the Name

We need to understand that the enemy will come in and try to take over our lives if we let him. If he can't get us to sin, he'll try to hinder us in some way. He might try to have our finances cut off or try to put some symptom of sickness on us. That's why we need to learn how to take authority over him in the Name of Jesus!

Now I'm not saying that we should go around looking for devils behind every bush and tree, so to speak. But we do need to understand that evil spirits exist. The most important thing we must understand is that we have the power over devils and demons in the Name of Jesus. And we need to understand that we have that power, not because of who we are, or how much faith we have, or how much we can pray in tongues. We have power and authority because of Jesus — because we have His Name.

As I said before, we can't take authority over the devil by praying in tongues. Tongues are primarily to keep oneself built up (1 Cor. 14:2,4; Jude 20). The Name of Jesus is the power we need when dealing with the enemy.

The Name of Jesus will work now just like it did in the Book of Acts. If you read the Book of Acts, you'll notice that the disciples used the Name of Jesus in deliverance (Acts 16:18). In the Epistles, you will find that Paul used the Name in deliverance (Eph. 1:18-23; Phil. 2:10).

There is such a thing as true deliverance, and the devil knows that. That's why he has tried to get that doctrine twisted and turned around so Christians will get into excess and error concerning deliverance. Many times, people are afraid to say anything about deliverance. That's exactly what the devil wants. Because the devil is real, and he will try to steal, kill, and destroy a person's life if he can. So we need to be aware of that fact and understand the truth about how to come against him in the Name of Jesus and stop him in his tracks!

We don't have to be afraid of the devil; we have authority over him in the Name of Jesus! We don't have to have all-night prayer meetings; we have *the Name!*

I have actually heard about someone who said, "I had 145 demons in me. It took fourteen days to get them all cast out."

Do you know what I said when I heard that? I said, "It took Jesus less than a minute to cast out two thousand" (Mark 5:1-13)!

Years ago, one of our RHEMA short-term missions teams was in India ministering. In one meeting, a demon-possessed girl came running to the platform and fell down, rolling around and slithering like a snake.

The minister who was preaching simply said, "In the Name of Jesus, be delivered." He didn't even lay hands on the demon-possessed girl. He didn't call a prayer meeting. He didn't carry on a conversation with the devil, asking how many spirits there were. He just used his authority in the Name!

The following day, this girl came back to the meetings. The minister told me that no one recognized her! She was completely restored in that Name!

We'll never have to be defeated again in life when we understand the power that's in the Name of Jesus! No matter what the problem, the Bible says that everything in Heaven, earth, and under the earth has to bow to the sound of that majestic Name. That means that whatever you're facing, if it has a name, it has to bow to the Name above every name, the Name of Jesus!

Rise Up Out of Defeat
And Into Victory — in the Name

You may feel defeated and hemmed-in by the power of the adversary. But you can rise up in the almighty Name of Jesus! You can use that Name to hurl back enemy forces! You can take your deliverance, victory, and freedom, by taking your authority — in the Name of Jesus! Whatever it is that you need to take authority over in your life, just raise your hands and begin to thank God for the Name of Jesus!

Then *use* your authority! Talk to your situation. Speak to it in the Name of Jesus. Tell the devil that he must turn loose of your finances. Tell him that he has to stop harassing your mind! Then thank the Father in the Name of Jesus that His Word is true and that the situation is taken care of. It's all in the Name!

For a more in-depth study of the operation of demons and evil spirits, *see* Rev. Kenneth E. Hagin's book *The Triumphant Church: Dominion Over All the Powers of Darkness.*

Chapter 8
Bearing Fruit in the Name

> *I am the vine, ye are the branches: He that abideth in me, and I in him, the same bringeth forth much fruit: for without me ye can do nothing . . . .*
>
> *Herein is my Father glorified, THAT YE BEAR MUCH FRUIT; so shall ye be my disciples.*
>
> — John 15:5,8

I once read that there are about 140 scriptures in the New Testament that tell us who we are, what we are, and what we have in Christ. So in a study of the Name of Jesus, it would be good for you to take a close look at who you are in Him.

As you read the New Testament, and especially the Epistles, you'll see phrases such as "in Him," "in whom," "through whom," and so forth that speak of your position as a believer. Those passages speak of your union with Him and your legal standing and place in the family of God.

As believers, we are "in Christ," so we have His Name. Through our union with Him, we can take

161

that Name and bear much fruit for the Kingdom of God.

We Are Christ's Representatives

God has made tremendous benefits available to those who are born again — to those who are *in Him*. In Him, we have a right to use His Name. We could say it like this: Those of us who are born again have been authorized to be His representatives on the earth.

Have you ever been employed by a company to act as that company's representative at certain functions or events? Maybe you currently represent your company as a salesman. If you do, or if you've ever been some kind of representative, you know about the *authorization* or *permission* you are given to represent something or someone else.

At RHEMA Bible Church, for example, several people on staff carry cards that tell others who we are — what our titles are as representatives of RHEMA Bible Church. Those cards authorize us to do the job we're supposed to do.

Our associate pastors have cards that can get them into hospitals to visit church members at certain times and places others might not be allowed to visit. They can show hospital personnel their card — their authorization — and that card gives them the authority to be there and to do their job as a pastor.

Also, our pastoral staff has to follow certain regulations to obtain the necessary authorization to go into jails and prisons. The purpose of this authorization is to show that the pastor is a bona fide representative of our church.

Have you ever seen a sign on a door in a hospital, bank, or some other corporation that read "Authorized Personnel Only"? Those signs mean that only those with the proper identification or authorization may pass through those doors.

I hope these examples give you a better picture of who we are in Christ as His representatives or ambassadors (2 Cor. 5:20). We are Jesus' representatives here on the earth! And because we are His representatives, we have certain authorization. What authorization is that? *The authorization to use His Name and to bear much fruit through our union with Him.*

Now let me say this so you won't misunderstand me: As Jesus' representatives, we certainly aren't gods. We aren't even *little* gods! We are Jesus' representatives, but to get carried away and say that we are divine, in the same sense that He is, causes problems. We aren't diety. But we are joint-heirs with Jesus Christ (Rom. 8:17). And because we are joint-heirs, we are sent forth in this earth to work on His behalf. Jesus is the Head. We, the Church of the Lord Jesus Christ, are His Body.

I think I know how some may have been led to believe that we are deity. For example, First John 4:17 says, *"Herein is our love made perfect, that we may have boldness in the day of judgment: because AS HE IS, SO ARE WE IN THIS WORLD."* (I'll talk more about this verse later.) But as I said before, we are ambassadors, not deity.

If you've ever read a contract or legal document, you know that if you were to change the wording just a little bit, you would change the meaning also. The legal interpretation of that document would be different.

Sometimes I think that is true in Christian circles concerning the way we word things. Much of what we call doctrinal differences is just a matter of semantics or the way something is said. In other words, most of the people who quote scriptures such as First John 4:17, don't really believe we are deity or little gods. But because of the way they express themselves, one could be led to think they do believe that.

Now look at another passage that illustrates our union with Christ and our rights as His representatives to use His Name.

2 CORINTHIANS 6:14-16
**14 Be ye not unequally yoked together with unbe-
lievers: for what fellowship hath righteousness
with unrighteousness? and what communion hath
light with darkness?**
**15 And what concord hath Christ with Belial? or
what part hath he that believeth with an infidel?**
**16 And what agreement hath the temple of God with
idols? for ye are the temple of the living God; as God
hath said, I will dwell in them, and walk in them;
and I will be their God, and they shall be my people.**

In this passage, the believer is simply told not
to be unequally yoked with unbelievers. In verse
14, believers are called "righteous"; unbelievers are
called "*un*righteous." Believers are called "light";
unbelievers are called "*darkness.*"

Then in verse 15, Paul asks, ". . . *what concord
hath CHRIST with BELIAL? or what part hath HE
THAT BELIEVETH with an INFIDEL?*"

Identified With Christ

In this verse, believers are called "Christ,"
meaning we are identified with Him! Why? Because
we are His representatives on the earth. Christ is
the Head; we are the Body. We are one with
Christ — joint-heirs with Him — joined with Him
in a living union. We aren't gods, but *we have been*

given the right to use the Name of Jesus and to act on His behalf!

Jesus was telling us in modern language, "Take My Name; be My representative." Christ, with His resurrected flesh-and-bone body, is at the right hand of God. We are here, on the earth, as His representatives. And we are His representatives, not only collectively — as the Church — but *individually*.

You see, as a corporate, collective body, we are the Body of Christ, and we have the right to use His Name. But we *also* have the right to use His Name individually.

We need to understand who we are in Christ and that we have a right to the Name of Jesus because of who we are in Him. Apart from Him, we can do nothing (John 15:5). Unless a person is really grounded in the Scriptures, he could get offtrack and become confused concerning some of the teachings we've heard that we are little gods.

But it doesn't matter who teaches what! What matters is what the *Bible* says! The Apostle Paul didn't say, "If I or an angel or an emissary from Heaven come teaching any other Gospel, *grab hold of it and run off with it.*" No! He said, *"But though we, or an angel from heaven, preach any other gospel unto you than that which we have preached*

unto you, let him be accursed" (Gal. 1:8). In other
words, don't have anything to do with it!

Now look at First John 4:17 again.

> **1 JOHN 4:17**
> **17 Herein is our love made perfect, that we may
> have boldness in the day of judgment: because as
> he is, so are we in this world.**

As He is, so are we in this world! Well, who is
"He"? "He" is Jesus! The following verse gives us
some idea of how we are to represent Him in this
world.

> **HEBREWS 13:8**
> **8 Jesus Christ the same yesterday, and to day, and
> for ever.**

The reason we are representatives of Jesus in the
earth is that He is physically at the right hand of the
Father on High. He completed His earthly ministry
in the flesh when He was crucified at Calvary. But
Hebrews 13:8 says that Jesus Christ is the same yesterday, today, and forever. Since that is true, then
Jesus is still willing to heal, deliver, and set free all
who are bound today — just as He was willing to
heal, deliver, and set free when He walked on the
earth.

What did Jesus do when He was on the earth?

ACTS 10:38
**38 How God anointed Jesus of Nazareth with the
Holy Ghost and with power: who went about
DOING GOOD, and HEALING ALL THAT WERE
OPPRESSED OF THE DEVIL; for God was with
him.**

What are we to do on this earth as Jesus' representatives? *We are to take His Name and do as He
did in this world!* In this world, Jesus "*. . . went
about doing good, and healing all that were
oppressed of the devil . . . .*" That's why He gave us
His Name and the authorization to use that
Name — to do what He did on the earth. John 14:12
says, "*. . . He that believeth on me, the works that I
do shall he do also; and greater works than these
shall he do; because I go unto my Father.*"

So as representatives of Jesus, we are to point
people to Him and introduce them to Jesus our Savior, Deliverer, Healer, and Baptizer! This is part of
the fruit we are to bear in His Name!

Whatever the need of mankind, Jesus can meet
it. He paid the price in His death, burial, and resurrection. And we have His Name. We aren't supposed
to be walking around, conquered and beat down. We
are supposed to be walking around in His Name,
doing what He did when He was on earth. That's

why He gave us His Name! And as He is, so are we in this world!

The *New International Version* of First John 4:17 says, "Love is made complete among us so that we will have confidence on the day of judgment, because in this world we are like him." And we know that Jesus is the same right now as He was yesterday. In Mark chapter 10, Bartimaeus said, "Have mercy on me." Jesus said, "What do you want?" The blind man replied, "I want to see." So Jesus said, "You've got it" (vv. 46-52).

Jesus hasn't changed. He is still willing to heal and meet the needs of all who call upon Him.

We Must Have His Compassion To Bear Fruit in His Name

Now let's look at something else in connection with our union with Jesus in the earth. It says in many places in the Gospels that Jesus was moved with compassion. So if we are His representatives — if we are going to be like Him in this earth — then we must also have compassion.

Compassion is something that so many in the Church don't have. But Jesus gave us the power to do good, and to be moved with compassion in His name. Because we are in Him!

When you're moved with compassion for someone, your prayer for them is different. It's not a cold, dry, apathetic prayer. No, it's fervent and heartfelt.

John G. Lake was an apostle of faith to South Africa at the turn of the century. In five years' time, Lake built five hundred churches in that nation.

Lake related one incident in which the wife of one of the leading government officials was dying with terminal cancer. She'd been taking a lot of drugs for pain, which kept her sort of "knocked out." Finally, she made the personal decision, "I'm not going to take these drugs anymore. I'm going to believe God for my healing."

So Lake told her, "If that's your stand — if that's what you want — we'll stand with you." Then he organized a group of believers — including himself, other ministers, and laypersons — to remain constantly at her bedside praying. Twenty-four hours a day, someone was there praying for this woman. That's the only way she could get any rest, because she was in so much pain. But when people prayed, she would get relief and fall asleep.

(Years ago, when I was an associate pastor for my father-in-law in Garland, Texas, there was a woman in the church who had cancer. Sometimes she would call me three or four times a night to pray for her.

She said that when I prayed, the pain would subside, and she could go to sleep for a couple of hours or so.

Someone asked, "Didn't you get tired of doing that?" No, I didn't get tired of it. If it helped her get some relief from her pain, I was always ready to minister to her. You've got to have compassion if you're going to minister to others effectively.)

One morning after Lake organized the prayer vigil for this official's wife who had cancer, he went home to bathe and change clothes before heading back to the sick woman's house. Then on his way back, within two blocks of the woman's house, he heard the woman screaming out in pain.

Lake wrote that when he heard the woman screaming, he became overwhelmed with compassion and he began running toward her house. Without realizing what he was doing, he ran into the woman's room where she and the others were. He picked up the woman's emaciated, practically lifeless body, in his arms and began to weep with godly compassion. And while he was weeping, the woman was completely healed!

We not only have the authority Jesus gave us, we also have His compassion. And as He is, so are we in this world (1 John 4:17)! That's why we need to understand the Name of Jesus and the power therein. We need to understand who we are in Christ and what kind of representative we are supposed to be. I'm not talking about just preachers! I'm talking about all those who've been born again by the blood of the Lord Jesus Christ. The *Church*, His Body, has been given His Name. We are one with Him. I want you to notice what Jesus said about this in John 17.

> **JOHN 17:23**
> 23 I [Jesus] **in them, and thou in me, that they may be made perfect in one; and that the world may know that thou hast sent me, and hast loved them, as thou hast loved me.**

What was Jesus saying here? He was praying for all believers everywhere in verses 20 and 26. Then in verse 23, He prayed to the Father, ". . . *that the world may know that thou hast sent me, and hast LOVED THEM, AS thou hast LOVED ME.*"

You see, the Father loves us *as* He loves Jesus! The understanding of that will change the believer's life! Yet some say, "I wish I could really believe that."

Well, look at Second Corinthians 5:17 and 21.

> **2 CORINTHIANS 5:17,21**
> 17 **Therefore if any man be in Christ, he is a new creature: old things are passed away; behold, all things are become new . . . .**
> 21 **For he hath made him [Jesus] to be sin for us, who knew no sin; that we might be made the righteousness of God in him.**

This Scripture passage says that we who are born again — new creatures in Christ — are the righteousness of God in Christ. You see, some Christians are always trying to *become* righteous. It's a waste of time, though, for a Christian to try to become righteous when he already *is* righteous. In the New Birth, he becomes the righteousness of God in Christ. Yet you still hear some Christians saying, "Well, I'm just trying to be righteous."

New Creation Realities

I think righteousness is one of the most misunderstood subjects in the Bible. But the truth of the matter is, a person is either righteous or he is not!

Let me explain. In general, a person is a male or female because he or she is born that way. For example, a person of the male gender was *born* a male. So he doesn't have to try to become more of a male, because he already *is* male!

Similarly, how did you as a Christian get to be righteous? You were born that way in the New Birth! It's so simple, yet man has tried to make it complicated. Theologians use big terms and complicated phrases that try to explain the New Birth, but the Bible explains it best: ". . . *if any man be in Christ, he is a NEW CREATURE: old things are passed away; behold, all things are become new"* (2 Cor. 5:17).

So the New Birth isn't hard to understand if we'll just believe the Bible. The things of God aren't hard to understand.

So get hold of this explanation of righteousness! You are born into righteousness just like you were born male or female. This makes righteousness very easily understood! And because you are born righteous, you can't become any more righteous than you can become more male if you're male, or more female if you're female. In the Name of Jesus, you were *born* righteous! You *are* righteous — in Him!

Righteousness means *right-standing with God.* It's that simple, because the *Gospel* is simple! We are born unto righteousness or right-standing with God, and we have been given the power of attorney or the authorization to use the Name of Jesus Christ as His representatives in this earth.

In one Gospel account, Jesus said, "I need to be about My Father's business" (Luke 2:49). And as He is, so are we in this world. We are the righteousness of God in Christ, so we need to be about the Father's business, bearing much fruit in His Name!

You need to say that out loud to yourself: "I am the righteousness of God in Christ. I am Christ's representative, an ambassador of Christ, in this world. And in His Name, I can be about my Father's business and bear much fruit."

Let that be a reality on the inside of you. When you understand that you *are* the righteousness of God in Christ, you will be about your Father's business, doing the works of Jesus on the earth.

When you get hold of the reality of your union with Christ, you will use your God-given authority to take your place as a new creature in Christ and as a representative of Jesus on the earth. Then when you are in a place where devils and demons are operating through someone, such as a mission field, you won't try to have some long, drawn-out prayer service. No, you'll stand in front of the person, look him straight in the eye, and say, "In the Name of Jesus Christ, be delivered!" And you will see that person change before your eyes.

The power is in the Name of Jesus. Again, I thank God for fasting and prayer. But when you're in a service, and a demon-possessed person starts interrupting the service, you don't have time to call a four-hour "praying-in-tongues service." It wouldn't do the demon-possessed person any good anyway. No, you step out in the Name of Jesus and demonstrate the power of God in that Name.

Do you know what brings crowds to church? *Demonstrations of the power of God in the Name of Jesus.* A pastor doesn't have to launch a major ad campaign or get on the radio and television. If he understands the Name of Jesus and teaches his people that they are the righteousness of God in Christ, his people will bear much fruit and his church will grow.

As I said, we are one with Christ; we are in union with Him. And our continued union with Christ enables us to bear fruit for the Kingdom of God. Look at what Jesus said in John chapter 15.

> **JOHN 15:5,8**
> **5 I am the vine, ye are the branches: HE THAT ABIDETH IN ME, and I IN HIM, the same bringeth forth much fruit . . . .**
> **8 Herein is my Father glorified, that ye bear much fruit . . . .**

The Life Is in the Vine

When Jesus said, "I am the Vine; you are the branches" (John 15:5), He was probably referring figuratively to a grapevine. I have seen a grape vineyard and have picked ripe grapes off the vines.

When I first saw a grapevine, I didn't look at the vine as being separate from the branches on the vine. I didn't differentiate between them at all. In the same way, we are one with Christ! He is the Vine; we are the branches. We are in union with Him.

Similarly, when you look at a fruit tree, you don't look at the branches as being one thing and the tree trunk as something else entirely, do you? No, you look at the tree as a whole. You call the entire thing a tree. You don't say, "Oh, look, there's a trunk with some branches on it" or "There are some branches with some fruit on them." No, you'd probably say, "Look at the fruit on that tree."

Whether you're talking about a grapevine or a fruit tree, fruit grows on branches. And on a grapevine, fruit is produced on the branches, but the fruit only grows on the branches because of the life that's in the *vine*.

Jesus is the Vine. And from the life we receive from Him, we, the branches, are supposed to bear much fruit. So He said, *"I am the vine, ye are the branches: He that abideth in me, and I in him, the same bringeth forth much fruit: for without me ye can do nothing"* (John 15:5). We are supposed to bear fruit from the life we receive from Jesus, the Vine.

What fruit are we to bear? *Doing the works of Jesus.* What are the works of Jesus? We read that everywhere He went, He was doing good and healing all that were oppressed of the devil (Acts 10:38). So that's what we're supposed to be doing in His Name! We are His representatives, and in His Name, we are to go forth and do the works that He did when He was on the earth.

Faith and the Name

Now many people say, "Well, we've got to have faith to use that Name." But have you ever noticed how little faith is mentioned in connection with the Name of Jesus. Jesus simply told us that He was giving us His Name, and He delegated to us His authority. So the ultimate power is in His Name, not in how much faith we have.

Now, of course anyone who knows me knows I'm not against faith. We have to have faith to receive other things from the Word of God. The Bible says that without faith, it is impossible to please God (Heb. 11:6). But you don't have to wait for something you already have if you are a believer and you have been given use of the Name.

To illustrate this point, suppose you had a thousand dollars in the bank. Do you think you would need a lot of faith to use that money? No. If you needed it, you would just use it! Why? Because it's your money; it belongs to you. And you have a right to use what belongs to you.

The Name of Jesus belongs to us, and we have a right to use His Name. At the mention of that Name, not according to how much faith you have, everything in Heaven, in earth, and under the earth has to bow its knee.

Some people try to complicate faith when it is really very simple. For example, when you have faith in something or someone, you will rest and trust that everything's taken care off — and that everything's going to be all right. So faith is normal in children who have loving parents that provide for them. Those children never worry about where their next meal is coming from! They don't come inside every few minutes, asking, "Mamma, if I ask you for a slice of bread, you'll give me bread, right?" No, they know they can have bread and whatever else they need. They automatically act on that fact.

When I was a young adult my mom told me, "Son, there's the kitchen. Anything that's in there, you can have it to eat if you want it." I didn't have to go beg and plead again and again. All I had to do was go in the kitchen and get some food!

Usually, I was hungry when I came home from school. I had the attitude, *If it's there, I'm going to eat it. If Mom or Patsy don't want me to eat it, they'd better put a sign on it that says, "Do not eat this!"*

When I was in high school, I was as tall as I am now, but I only weighed 145 pounds. My daddy used to say that I had two hollow legs, because I ate so much! Even if we were going to eat supper just a few hours later, I'd eat after school and at suppertime too! And I probably drank a quart of milk while I was doing it. What's more, I didn't gain weight eating like that! (I wish that were so now!)

The reason I helped myself to whatever I wanted to eat was because I was told it was mine for the taking. Well, spiritually, Jesus told us that His Name has been given to us and that we can use it! It's ours for the taking. So we don't have to wonder or worry about it — *it's ours!*

We Can Reign in Life Through the Name

As Christians, we are to rule and reign in life by Jesus Christ and by His Name.

ROMANS 5:17
17 For if by one man's offence death reigned by one; much more they which receive abundance of grace and of the gift of righteousness shall reign in life by one, Jesus Christ.

Now you could rephrase the first part of this scripture like this: "For if by Adam's offense, spiritual death came, that is, poverty, hatred, lying, sickness, and so forth. You name it — if it falls under the devil's category — it's there because of Adam's offense."

Now let's look at *The Amplified Bible* version.

> **ROMANS 5:17 (*Amplified*)**
> **17 For if, because of one man's trespass (lapse, offense) death reigned through that one, much more surely will those who receive [God's] overflowing grace (unmerited favor) and the free gift of righteousness (putting them into right standing with Himself) reign as kings in life through the One, Jesus Christ, the Messiah, the Anointed One.**

Both versions tell us that we are to rule and reign over poverty and sickness, and really, over *anything* that's of the devil, including strife between fellow Christians. Because Jesus won the victory over spiritual death.

So often, it's not "*people* problems" we have to deal with, it's "*devil* problems." If the devil would get his head out of the way, we wouldn't go against one another. We'd live in unity and harmony.

I pastor a multiracial church. People of many different races, nationalities, and backgrounds attend, and all of us work together for one cause — the

cause of the Lord Jesus Christ! Through the blood of
Jesus and through His Name, we are all brothers
and sisters. We are all a part of the family of God.

And we can reign in life through that Name! We
are more than conquerors (Rom. 8:37)! We don't
have to live on "Barely-Get-Along Street" right
beside "Grumble Alley," down the street from
"Gone-Gone Avenue!"

Some people actually think that's the way Christians are supposed to go through life — defeated
and downtrodden. They think that the poorer you
are, the more righteous and humble you are. They
think Christians are supposed to live with their
nose to the grindstone, the seat of their britches
patched up, the top of their hat worn out, and the
soles of their shoes full of holes. They think they
have to drive an old beat-up car that backfires and
blows smoke everywhere.

Now don't misunderstand me. I'm not saying
that it's wrong to have an old car. Years ago, all I
had was a '65 Ford. On a cold morning, I had to
push it to start it, because the valves were so bad!
And at one time or another, most of us have driven
what I call a jalopy while we were believing God to
raise us up and prosper us. But when Christians
remain in poverty year after year, without their
needs being met, and believe they are being humble

and pious before God as a result, that doesn't paint an accurate picture of the life God wants His children to live. When some of those same Christians try to witness to a sinner and push that kind of believing off on him, most of the time, the sinner will say, *"No, thanks!"*

Our Inheritance in Christ

I'm not just preaching a "prosperity gospel"; I'm preaching *the* Gospel. Jesus said He came that we might have life and life more abundantly (John 10:10). That applies to our spiritual *and* natural lives. Bearing fruit in the Name includes appropriating the blessings and benefits God has provided for us in Christ. We are to live a victorious life!

So we need to learn to reign in life through the Name of Jesus and through the Word. We need to believe God's Word despite our circumstances and learn to rise above the circumstances — above sickness, disease, poverty, and defeat. Then when a sinner sees our changed lives (not just a change in our heart but change on the outside) they will want to know what happened. They'll start coming around and saying, "I want to get in on this!"

How do we take our places and reign in life? By getting into the Word and understanding who we

are in Christ and what we have in His Name. Then
we'll begin to bear fruit — to partake of the blessings and benefits God has provided for us in Him.

> **COLOSSIANS 1:12,13**
> **12 Giving thanks unto the Father, which HATH
> MADE US meet [or able] to be partakers of the
> inheritance of the saints in light:**
> **13 Who hath delivered us from the power of dark-
> ness, and hath translated us into the kingdom of
> his dear Son.**

This passage of Colossians tells us that God *has*
made us "meet" or *able* to be partakers of the inheritance of the saints! That's one reason to give
thanks unto the Father: We need to thank Him in
Jesus' Name for what He has provided for us — for
our inheritance!

What is our inheritance? Among other things, it
includes deliverance from the power and authority
of darkness — from demons, sickness, disease, and
poverty. God has delivered us from everything that
belongs under Satan's dominion. So instead of
Satan's reigning over *us, we* are to reign over *him.*

We can reign in life, not because of who we are in
ourselves but because of who we are in Christ. We
are one with Him. We have His Name. That's where
the power is; that's where the deliverance is; and
that's where the reigning in life is — in the Name!

So let us rise up and let us take advantage of what belongs to us, bearing much fruit to the glory of God!

Chapter 9
Salvation and the Name

When we use the word "salvation," we're usually talking about the New Birth and the remission of sin. But do you know, that's only *part* of salvation? Certainly, it's the most important part, but the word "salvation" itself entails more than that. The remission of sin is part of the package, and it's the *first* part of the package. But if you apply salvation only to the New Birth and the remission of sin, you limit God in what He can do for you.

We need to realize that we are the ones, not God, who put the limit on what we receive from Him. God doesn't limit us; we limit ourselves. When you read the Word, you'll find that through the Name of Jesus, unlimited resources belong to the Christian — to the one who's been born again.

Let's look further into the full meaning of the word "salvation."

ROMANS 1:16
16 For I am not ashamed of the gospel of Christ: for it is the power of God unto SALVATION to every one that believeth; to the Jew first, and also to the Greek.

187

In the margin of some Bibles, there's a little footnote next to the word "salvation" in this Romans verse. It says, in essence, "The Hebrew and Greek words for salvation imply the idea of *deliverance, safety, preservation, healing,* and *soundness.*"

The Scofield Bible says, "Salvation is a great inclusive word of the Gospel, gathering unto itself all the redemptive acts and processes."

Wow! From reading that, we can begin to understand why we need to study and become familiar with the full meaning of the word "salvation." Thank God that salvation includes the remission and forgiveness of sin, but it includes many other benefits!

PSALM 103:2
2   Bless the Lord, O my soul, and forget not all his BENEFITS.

You see, this verse in Psalms is talking about what Scofield called "all the redemptive acts and processes." Of course, we know that the most important aspect of our redemption is the remission of sin. In fact, you can't get in on most of the benefits of God's Word until you have been saved. But once you've been saved, you have an inclusive term "salvation" that encompasses more than the remission of sin. There are many more benefits besides that, so the Psalmist exhorted us not to forget them!

Romans 1:16 says, *"For I am not ashamed of the gospel of Christ: for it is the power of God unto SAL-VATION to every one that believeth; to the Jew first, and also to the Greek."* We could read that verse: "The Gospel of Christ is the power of God unto *deliverance"* or "The Gospel of Christ is the power of God unto *safety"* or "The Gospel of Christ is the power of God unto *preservation"* or "The Gospel of Christ is the power of God unto *healing"* or "The Gospel of Christ is the power of God unto *soundness!"*

As I said, if we limit God by only applying salvation to the New Birth and the remission of sin, we won't be able to receive the rest of what salvation stands for — *deliverance, safety, preservation, soundness,* and *healing.* That's what the enemy would like us to do. If He can get us to stop at the New Birth, he can rob us of receiving the rest of the inheritance that belongs to us in the Name of Jesus. What does that inheritance include? It includes the remission of sin, the forgiveness of sin, and healing and health for our physical bodies. Let's look at each of these benefits briefly.

The Remission of Sin in the Name

Second Corinthians 5:17 says, *"Therefore if any man be in Christ, he is a new creature: old things are passed away; behold, all things are become new."*

This verse tells us, *old things are passed away.* These "old things" are the sinful life and every sin we committed before we surrendered to God. And do you know what? When those things are "passed away," God doesn't remember them!

> **ISAIAH 43:25**
> **25** I [God the Father], **even I, am he that blotteth out thy transgressions for mine own sake, and WILL NOT REMEMBER THY SINS.**

> **MICAH 7:19**
> **19** He [God the Father] **will turn again, he will have compassion upon us; he will subdue our iniquities; and thou wilt CAST ALL THEIR SINS INTO THE DEPTHS OF THE SEA.**

This verse in Micah is where we get the saying that when we repent, "all of our sins are cast into the sea of forgetfulness." Have you ever heard that statement? There's no scripture that actually talks about the sea of forgetfulness, but if you take the essence of both of these scriptures, you could easily see the truth of that statement.

I've heard people say things, such as, "Your sins have been taken away," "Your sins have been cast into the sea of forgetfulness," and "God doesn't remember your sins." Well, if you've repented in the Name of Jesus, then according to the Word of God, those statements are true!

Nazi Concentration Camp Survivor

I like what Corrie Ten Boom added concerning sins that God has "cast into the depths of the sea." She said "So don't go fishing for them!" I like that! In other words, she was saying, "Leave those sins alone! As far as God is concerned, they don't exist anymore! The blood of Jesus has cleansed them, and they don't exist!"

Psalm 103:12 paints another beautiful picture of how God regards sin for which we've repented.

> **PSALM 103:12**
> 12 As far as the east is from the west, so far hath he [God] removed our transgressions from us.

"As far as the east is from the west" is a distance that's immeasurable! Think about it. If you started traveling east and kept on traveling, it wouldn't matter how long you kept traveling — days, weeks, months, or *years* — you would still be traveling east! In other words, the points east and west never meet!

I'm glad the Lord said, "As far as the east is from the west" instead of "As far as the north is from the south." Why? Because if you were to travel north and continue traveling north, then when you reached the North Pole, and continued your northward direction, you would automatically begin heading south! So the points north and south do meet, but east and west *never* meet! (Hold on to that truth a while, and the truth about the remission of sin will become a greater reality to you.)

In Jesus' death on the Cross, He bore our sins and took them away from us. That becomes a reality in our lives individually when we become born again — when we accept Jesus Christ as Savior and receive the remission of sin. At that point, in our own lives, God removes our transgressions from us as far as the east is from the west (Ps. 103:12)!

But the devil will try to bring up your past sins, because if he can hold you under condemnation, you won't be able to boldly demand your rights as a Christian in the Name of Jesus. The devil will try to bring you a "photograph" of what you've done in the past (it can only be a "photograph," because the actual sin doesn't exist anymore). So to be able to stand against and defeat the enemy, you will have to know that your sin doesn't exist anymore as far as God is concerned. God has already blotted it out. Jesus dealt with the sin problem. He took it away from us. Our sin is in the sea of forgetfulness!

As I said, all the devil can do is bring you a picture of what you did in the past, but it's only a picture. For example, if you have a photograph of yourself, you know that photograph isn't the real you; it's only a *picture* of you. And if it's a very old photograph, you probably don't even look the same anymore. Why? Because you've changed; you're not the same person.

I recently saw some pictures of me in an old RHEMA Bible Training Center brochure. I hardly recognized myself! My hair used to be solid black — down in Texas, we say "coal-black"! But it's not that way anymore. Now I've only got a little black hair to go with the grey!

Those pictures of me in that old brochure were images of me from a long time ago. In much the same way, the picture of your past that Satan tries to bring you is only an image of you before you became a new creature in Christ. Therefore, that picture doesn't even represent the real you. So you can laugh at Satan and say, "I don't know why you're bringing that photo around here. The person in that photo is *'dead.'* I am now alive in Jesus Christ!"

In the Name of Jesus, you can run Satan off, saying, "Take your picture and all your condemnation and get out of here, Mr. Devil, in the Name of Jesus!"

Forgiveness in the Name

"Yes," someone said, "that's just wonderful. But what happens if we sin after we're already saved?"

Jesus took care of that too.

1 JOHN 1:9
9   If we confess our sins, he is faithful and just to forgive us our sins, and to cleanse us from all unrighteousness.

Now some use this scripture for the sinner, but, really, it doesn't apply to the sinner; it applies to the Christians. After you become a Christian, the minute you do something wrong, you know it. Your heart will condemn you. That's what First John 1:9 is for — so a Christian can immediately ask for and receive forgiveness. Now you're not to go out with the *intention* of committing sin. But if you do sin, you have an "escape clause" in First John 1:9. And after awhile, if you keep growing in grace and in the knowledge of God, you won't be making all the mistakes that you made to start with.

An older adult can remember back when he first started learning how to be an adult and can recall how he made quite a few mistakes. (If you didn't make mistakes, you were an exception to the rule.) For example, in managing your own finances, you probably didn't know everything you know now. You may have had to learn the hard way how to live on a budget and how to use credit properly.

When young people graduate from high school, they usually walk across a stage or platform, shake the hand of the school principal or superintendent, and receive their diploma. When they return to their seats after that handshake, in a sense, they go from being a kid to being an adult. From then on, the world and everyone around them expects more out of them. But going from adolescence to adulthood is not always a smooth transition, and mistakes are usually made along the way. Then gradually, those young adults grow and mature and learn how not to make so many mistakes.

The same is true with spiritual growth and maturity. A Christian at various levels of maturity usually doesn't *intend* to make mistakes. Nevertheless, he often does. And when he does, he has First John 1:9. As he appropriates that verse by confessing and receiving forgiveness for sin, he can continue moving on with God and maturing spiritually.

Just because a Christian makes a mistake doesn't mean the Spirit of God leaves him. A Christian who misses it and sins doesn't have to get saved all over again. Now if he leaves "Father's house" like the prodigal son, and gets into riotous living (Luke 15:11-24), then, I believe he should come back and rededicate himself to God in the Name of Jesus. But, thank God, he can come back.

And God forgives, just like the father did in the account of the prodigal son. Then he can go on, as though his sin never existed.

If you're a parent, one of your children has probably come to you and said, "I messed up; I made a mistake. I want you to forgive me." Usually, this happens with older kids.

My own children have said that to me. And I have always answered, "Yes, I'll forgive you." In most cases, I said, "You already understand your mistake. There's no use in my meting out any punishment, because you realize what you've done, and I don't believe you'll make that mistake again."

That's what God is saying to us! When we understand what we've done wrong and ask Him to forgive us, He says, "I forgive you. Now go on down the road, serving Me and walking with Me."

There's remission and forgiveness of sin in the Name of Jesus!

Healing in the Name

You know, you can ask some Christians, "Does the Name of Jesus belong to the Church?" and they'll answer, "Yes." Then if you ask them, "What is that Name good for? What does the Name do?" they'll say, "Oh, His Name is just to be adored. It is to be praised. It is to be honored." That's just about all they think the Name of Jesus is for!

Don't misunderstand me, the Name of Jesus *is* to be adored, praised, and honored. But there's more to it than that. Jesus didn't just give us His Name so we could say, "Oh, praise the Lord. Praise the Name of Jesus." No, He gave it to us to use as His representatives on the earth.

The *Name* of Jesus represents the *Person* of Jesus — today, not just the Jesus of the Gospels two thousand years ago during His earthly ministry.

What do we know about the Person of Jesus from reading the Gospels? We know that while He was on the earth, He preached, He taught, and He healed.

And we know that *there's healing in the Name of Jesus!* Because Jesus said, ". . . *In my name . . . they shall lay hands on the sick, and they shall recover"* (Mark 16:17,18).

Peter and John understood the power in Jesus' Name to heal. Look at Acts chapter 3.

ACTS 3:1-8 (*NIV*)
1 One day Peter and John were going up to the temple at the time of prayer — at three in the afternoon.
2 Now a man crippled from birth was being carried to the temple gate called Beautiful, where he

was put every day to beg from those going into the
temple courts.
3   When he saw Peter and John about to enter, he
asked them for money.
4   Peter looked straight at him, as did John. Then
Peter said, "Look at us!"
5   So the man gave them his attention, expecting
to get something from them.
6   Then Peter said, "Silver or gold I do not have,
but what I have I give you. In the name of Jesus
Christ of Nazareth, walk."
7   Taking him by the right hand, he helped him
up, and instantly the man's feet and ankles became
strong.
8   He jumped to his feet and began to walk. Then
he went with them into the temple courts, walking
and jumping, and praising God.

I want you to notice that Peter said, ". . . what I
have I give you . . ." (v. 6). The *King James Version*
says, ". . . *such as I have give I thee . . . .*" Then it
goes on to say, ". . . *In the name of Jesus Christ of
Nazareth, rise up and walk*"!

We often talk about praying for the sick, but
notice Peter didn't even pray for this man! He just
said, "In the Name of Jesus Christ of Nazareth, rise
and be healed."

Many people have noted that in Brother Hagin's
healing lines, he just goes down the line, laying
hands on people and saying, "In the Name of
Jesus." He doesn't have to pray for them; they come

down to the altar in the first place to receive healing. So he ministers healing to them.

Sometimes Brother Hagin goes down the heal-
ing line, just saying, "In the Name. In the Name.
In the Name." What Name is he talking about?
The Name of Jesus!

After the healing of the crippled man in the
Book of Acts, Peter and John were taken into custody and "called on the carpet," so to speak, for
administering healing in the Name of Jesus. Peter
and John were called upon to give an account of
what happened.

> **ACTS 4:5-12 (NIV)**
> **5 The next day the rulers, elders and teachers of
> the law met in Jerusalem.**
> **6 Annas the high priest was there, and so were
> Caiaphas, John, Alexander and the other men of
> the high priest's family.**
> **7 They had Peter and John brought before them
> and began to question them: "By what power or
> what name did you do this?"**
> **8 Then Peter, filled with the Holy Spirit, said to
> them: "Rulers and elders of the people!**
> **9 If we are being called to account today for an
> act of kindness shown to a cripple and are asked
> how he was healed,**
> **10 then know this, you and all the people of Israel:
> It is by the name of Jesus Christ of Nazareth,
> whom you crucified but whom God raised from
> the dead, that this man stands before you healed.**

11 He is 'the stone you builders rejected, which has become the capstone.'
12 Salvation is found in no one else, for there is no other name under heaven given to men by which we must be saved."

So, you see, not only is there the remission and forgiveness of sin in the Name of Jesus, there's healing in the Name of Jesus too!

We need to know that healing for our physical body is a part of the Gospel of the Lord Jesus Christ. He not only took our sins, He also took our infirmities and bare our sicknesses.

ISAIAH 53:4,5
4   Surely he hath borne our griefs [the margin of some Bibles reads "sicknesses"], **and carried our sorrows** [the margin of some Bibles reads "pains"]: **yet we did esteem him stricken, smitten of God, and afflicted.**
5   But he was wounded for our transgressions, he was bruised for our iniquities: the chastisement of our peace was upon him; and with his stripes we are healed.

MATTHEW 8:17
17 That it might be fulfilled which was spoken by Esaias the prophet, saying, Himself took our INFIRMITIES, and bare our SICKNESSES.

In the Epistles, Peter renders it like this:

1 PETER 2:24
**24 Who his own self bare our sins in his own body
on the tree, that we, being dead to sins, should live
unto righteousness: by whose stripes ye were
healed.**

Healed. By Jesus' stripes we *were* healed. In
other words, God provided us with healing through
His great plan of redemption. *He has already provided healing for us.* It's ours now, and it becomes
real to us — through the Name.

Remember Mark 16:17 and 18 says, *". . . In my
name . . . they shall lay hands on the sick, and they
shall recover."* Why? Because healing already
belongs to us; it's already been paid for. If we could
get people to realize that healing is a part of salvation just as the remission of sin is, it would put an
end to people's not believing in healing.

You see, that Name still has all the power it ever
did. If it didn't, then salvation, as we preach it, is
wrong. In other words, if the Name has lost its
power, then the sick can't be healed in the Name!
But we know that Jesus Christ is the same yesterday, today, and forever (Heb. 13:8), and that Name
will never lose its power to heal.

MARK 16:17,18
**17 And these signs shall follow them that believe;
IN MY NAME shall they cast out devils; they shall
speak with new tongues;**

18 They shall take up serpents; and if they drink any deadly thing, it shall not hurt them; THEY SHALL LAY HANDS ON THE SICK, AND THEY SHALL RECOVER.

We read from Isaiah 53:4 and 5, Matthew 8:17, and First Peter 2:24, that healing is part and parcel of redemption and salvation. So to preach salvation only from the standpoint of the remission and forgiveness of sin is to do God's people a disservice, because we're not telling them what else is included in salvation.

To Receive God's Benefits Is Our Responsibility

Yet many ministers want to stop with the remission and forgiveness of sin. They don't want to continue into healing, because they have a problem explaining certain things, such as why some people don't receive healing. But, you know, it's not our responsibility to explain why something doesn't happen. It's our responsibility to preach and teach the truth of God's Word.

Actually, most of time, the reason a person doesn't get healed is, he doesn't know how to *receive*. Many times, the person doesn't really believe for himself that healing belongs to him and that he can appropriate it for his body in the Name.

Also, I've seen people who've *said* they believed in healing and that they were believing God, but in their fight of faith, they got to the point where they tired of fighting the faith battle, and they thought, *It would be easier to just go on to Heaven.* So they just quit and gave up in their faith.

But remember, *God* doesn't quit. If there's a failure, it has to be on our part — on man's part — somewhere, because God never fails.

When people don't receive healing and go home to be with Jesus, I think we're too prone many times to want to come up with some answer as to why it happened. But why a person dies early in life is between him and the Lord. Deuteronomy 29:29 says, *"The secret things belong unto the Lord our God: but those things which are revealed belong unto us and to our children for ever . . . ."*

When someone doesn't receive healing and goes on to be with the Lord, we need to keep ever before us the fact that God is still God; His Word is true; He can't lie; and He can't fail!

We don't need to try to come up with pat answers as to why someone failed in his or her faith. Where the Word of God is concerned, we do need to be bold and unwavering, because God's Word is true, and God can't fail.

If we were taught about healing in the Name of Jesus like we are taught about the New Birth in the Name, there wouldn't be any doubt concerning the power of the Name to heal. We would unconsciously exercise faith in healing like we exercise faith for the remission of sin.

You see, Jesus dealt with the sin problem. He bore our sins. People believe that; they accept that with no problem whatsoever. But many people won't accept the fact that Jesus, in consummating God's great plan of redemption, also made a way for us to be healed and delivered!

The Power of the Name To Quicken

Romans 8:11 says, *"But if the Spirit of him that raised up Jesus from the dead dwell in you, he that raised up Christ from the dead shall also quicken your mortal bodies by his Spirit that dwelleth in you."* This verse is talking about quickening a believer's mortal body, not his spirit man. Sometimes I think people spiritualize the Scriptures too much.

The word "mortal" refers to *death-doomed*. Paul said, *"For which cause we faint not; but though our outward* [death-doomed] *man perish, yet the inward man is renewed day by day"* (2 Cor. 4:16). In other words, Paul was saying that while his *inward man*, his spirit, was *being renewed* day by day, his *outward man*, his mortal body, was *perishing* or *dying* day by day. So Romans 8:11 is talking about the Spirit's quickening our mortal body, not our spirit. What does "quicken" mean? It means *to make full of life.*

I want you to understand that through salvation, we get a whole lot more than just the remission and forgiveness of sin. If we need healing, we can receive healing in the Name. We can receive help for our physical bodies.

And, because Jesus gave us His Name to use in His absence after His death, burial, and resurrection, according to Romans 8:11, we can also be quickened in His Name.

Romans 8:11 isn't just talking about healing or about somebody's being sick. No, I believe it's also talking about a quickening for a mortal body that's simply tired.

Sometimes instead of saying, "Oh, I'm so tired. I'm so tired," just say, "In the Name of Jesus, the Spirit Who lives within me is quickening my mortal body. He quickens me right now!"

We have that right; we have that authority. So we need to *use* our authority and experience more of God's quickening power!

Confession and the Name

God stands ready to manifest Himself — His power — to us because of the Name of Jesus. So we need to cooperate with Him by confessing His Word and by holding fast to our confession in the Name of Jesus!

Now some will say, "Well, now, wait a minute. I don't know whether I believe in that confession business or not."

But let me ask you a question. If they're Christians, how in the world did they ever get saved if they don't believe in that "confession business?" Romans chapter 10 says:

> **ROMANS 10:9,10**
> **9 That if thou shalt CONFESS with thy mouth the Lord Jesus, and shalt believe in thine heart that God hath raised him from the dead, thou shalt be saved.**
> **10 For with the heart man believeth unto righteousness; and with the mouth CONFESSION is made unto salvation.**

There is no salvation without confession. There is no remission of sin — no New Birth — without confession. *Our Christian experience begins with confession.* And it continues with our confession of what God's Word says about us.

But according to Romans 10:9 and 10, it's not just confession that gets the job done. It's confession and *believing.*

Believing what? Believing God's Word!

Believe the Word, Not Someone Else's Experience

You see, many people are making confessions that are never going to come to pass, because even though they believe in confession, they're not really hooked up to God's Word. They're hooked up to something else, such as someone else's experience.

But in order for your confession to be effective and bring results, it has to be based on the Word of God, not on someone's experience. In other words, just because someone else confessed something from the Word and received it is no sign that you can receive the same kind of blessing by making the same confession. No, the Word has to be real to *you.* Your confession of faith in God's Word must be *personal.*

Let me share a true story with you to illustrate this point. Years ago, a student at RHEMA Bible Training Center heard a testimony of someone who was led by God to give his car away. The Lord consequently blessed the person with a brand-new vehicle!

Well, this RHEMA student heard that and thought, *He gave his car away and received a new car. I'm going to do the same thing.* So he did — he gave away his car — and at the end of the school year, he was still walking!

You see, that student didn't have anything to base his confession on except someone else's experience. Certainly, you can believe God in His Word to meet your needs and to provide you with a car. But you can't just give away your car, expecting God to give you a brand-new one — unless He tells you to do it!

That's where a lot of people miss it: They say, "Well, if God did it for them, He'll do it for me." But there's more to it than that. Yes, you have to use your faith in God's Word, but you also have to do what God tells *you* to do, not what He tells someone else to do.

Don't do something just because someone else did it. Someone told me one time, "Well, I'm going to sell my house and confess that God will give me a bigger and better one. My neighbor did that, and it worked. *I'm* going to do it too."

But I said, "Now wait a minute. Do you understand that your neighbor got a promotion and a raise? Can you afford the payment on the new house right now?"

Then I told the man, "The first thing you need to do is start confessing for a better job and more finances. Then you can get a bigger house."

Faith Failures

The reason there are so many "faith" failures is because people hear the faith message and run off with it before they fully understand it. They get only half the message, and their faith doesn't work. Then they become disappointed and disillusioned with the entire message of faith.

Naturally speaking, you should know that if a meal is really going to benefit you, it's got to be balanced. It has to contain portions of all the basic food groups to provide the proper nutrition to your body. And when you don't eat a balanced diet, over a period of time, it begins to show up in your body in various ways.

Spiritually, people do the same thing with the faith message. They just grab hold of what they like to eat and leave the rest behind. Then when every-thing doesn't work right for them, they say, "Well, that faith business just doesn't work!"

But none of that changes the fact that real faith always works if it's used in line with the Word of God.

Similarly, I think what has happened with the power in the Name of Jesus is, people have only understood half the message. They've understood the New Birth, but they haven't understood healing and the authority that we as believers have in that Name.

But when Christians get hold of the entire truth of the power that's in the Name of Jesus, it will rev-olutionize their lives. They'll begin to make confes-sions based on the Word, and their circumstances will change for the better!

Confession Basics

As I said, our Christian experience begins with confession. But the problem with the church world as a whole is, that's where we've stopped — at the beginning. So let's look at some confession truths beginning in Hebrews chapter 3.

HEBREWS 3:1
1   Wherefore, holy brethren, partakers of the heav-enly calling, consider the Apostle and High Priest of our profession [or confession] **. . . .**

In several Bible translations, that word "profession" is translated as *confession.* And in many other translations, you will find a footnote referring to the word "profession" as *confession.*

Now we have already seen that confession holds a place in the New Birth.

> **ROMANS 10:9,10**
> 9 That if thou shalt confess with thy mouth the Lord Jesus, and shalt believe in thine heart that God hath raised him from the dead, thou shalt be saved.
> 10 For with the heart man believeth unto righteousness; and with the mouth confession is made unto salvation.

With the mouth, confession is made unto salvation. But confession also holds a place in our daily walk with God. We are to "hold fast our confession" in our everyday life.

> **HEBREWS 4:14**
> 14 Seeing then that we have a high priest, that is passed unto the heavens, Jesus the Son of God, let us hold fast [our] profession.

> **HEBREWS 10:23**
> 23 Let us hold fast the profession of our faith without wavering; (for he is faithful that promised;).

We believed in our heart and confessed with our mouth to get saved. But "believing in our heart and confessing with our mouth" is the way we receive all of God's blessings and benefits. What are we to believe? We are to believe what the Word says about us, and we are to confess that. We are to say what Jesus says about us, confessing who we are in Christ Jesus.

So confession is very important in the life of the believer. The believer is to take hold of the truth of who he is in Christ and confess his rights and privileges in Him.

You see, all of our blessings are wrapped up in Jesus. Salvation — the remission of sin and everything that belongs to us after we are saved — is wrapped up in Jesus and His Name. Without Jesus' death on the Cross, without the redemptive plan that was put into action when He hung suspended between Heaven and earth, we have nothing. Everything that God has provided for us is wrapped up in the crucifixion and the resurrection of the Lord Jesus Christ.

Doubt Will Rob You of Your Inheritance

There are great blessings and benefits for those who have learned to use Jesus' Name, to confess who they are and what they have in Christ, and to put away all doubt concerning the integrity of His Word.

But doubt will rob you of your inheritance. *Doubt and fear build confusion, but confession in the Name of Jesus builds faith.*

Someone said, "When faith comes in the front door, doubt and fear go out the back door." Just as light and darkness can't exist together, neither can faith and doubt. You either have faith or you have doubt. You either have faith or you have fear. Fear and doubt go together. But faith comes in and runs these enemies out. You need to move on with God and confess your faith, not your doubt. What Jesus has promised in His Word, you can have in His Name. So use the Name to appropriate that which belongs to you!

Confessing God's Truth Effectively

To be effective, your confession must absolutely agree with the Word of God. After you have prayed in Jesus' Name, you are to hold fast your confession. So don't destroy the effects of your own prayer by negative, unbelieving confession.

The following is a good example of what we need to confess in the Name of Jesus — the Name above all Names.

"The Name of Jesus is above all names.

The Name of Jesus is greater than every name.

The Name of Jesus carries authority in Heaven, in earth, and under the earth.

The Name of Jesus carries authority at the throne of God.

The Name of Jesus gives me authority over all demons and evil spirits.

The Name of Jesus belongs to me today on earth.

Jesus is here to see that my prayer is heard and answered.

Jesus is here to honor what I say.

The Word says, 'If I ask anything in His Name, He will do it.'

His Name has authority.

Jesus has authorized me to use His Name against my enemies,
    against all of hell, against all demons,
    against sickness and disease,
    against oppression and depression.

So in the Name of Jesus, I'm free!

I declare my freedom today!

Jesus has set me free!

All that He has done — all that is done by His
   power — all of His authority and the might
   of all of His conquests
   are invested in that Name.

And that Name belongs to me.

I am *more* than a conqueror through Him that
   loved me
   and gave Himself for me.

So I take that Name and I walk victoriously
   every day — 365 days a year, twenty-four
   hours a day, sixty seconds every minute.

I walk victoriously all of the time in the Name
   of Jesus."

Chapter 10
Scriptures for Meditation

There are many scriptures in the Word of God that deal specifically with the Name of Jesus. I'll list several, but these don't come close to exhausting all that God's Word has to say on this important subject of *Jesus* — Name above all names!

MATTHEW 1:21
21 And she shall bring forth a son, and thou shalt call his name JESUS: for he shall save his people from their sins.

MATTHEW 1:23
23 Behold, a virgin shall be with child, and shall bring forth a son, and they shall call his name Emmanuel, which being interpreted is, God with us.

MATTHEW 1:24,25
24 Then Joseph being raised from sleep did as the angel of the Lord had bidden him, and took unto him his wife:
25 And knew her not till she had brought forth her firstborn son: and he called his name JESUS.

MATTHEW 10:22
22 And ye shall be hated of all men for my name's sake: but he that endureth to the end shall be saved.

MATTHEW 12:18,21
18 Behold my servant, whom I have chosen; my beloved, in whom my soul is well pleased: I will put my spirit upon him, and he shall shew judgment to the Gentiles . . . .
21 And in his name shall the Gentiles trust.

MATTHEW 18:5
5   And whoso shall receive one such little child in my name receiveth me.

MATTHEW 18:19,20
19 Again I say unto you, That if two of you shall agree on earth as touching any thing that they shall ask, it shall be done for them of my Father which is in heaven.
20 For where two or three are gathered together in my name, there am I in the midst of them.

MATTHEW 19:29
29 And every one that hath forsaken houses, or brethren, or sisters, or father, or mother, or wife, or children, or lands, for my name's sake, shall receive an hundredfold, and shall inherit everlasting life.

MARK 9:38-41
38 And John answered him, saying, Master, we saw one casting out devils in thy name, and he followeth not us: and we forbad him, because he followeth not us.
39 But Jesus said, Forbid him not: for there is no man which shall do a miracle in my name, that can lightly speak evil of me.
40 For he that is not against us is on our part.

41 For whosoever shall give you a cup of water to drink in my name, because ye belong to Christ, verily I say unto you, he shall not lose his reward.

MARK 16:17,18

17 And these signs shall follow them that believe; In my name shall they cast out devils; they shall speak with new tongues.

18 They shall take up serpents; and if they drink any deadly thing, it shall not hurt them; they shall lay hands on the sick, and they shall recover.

LUKE 10:17

17 And the seventy returned again with joy, saying, Lord, even the devils are subject unto us through thy name.

LUKE 24:46,47

46 ... Thus it is written, and thus it behoved Christ to suffer, and to rise from the dead the third day:

47 And that repentance and remission of sins should be preached in his name among all nations, beginning at Jerusalem.

JOHN 1:12

12 But as many as received him, to them gave he power to become the sons of God, even to them that believe on his name.

JOHN 2:23

23 Now when he was in Jerusalem at the passover, in the feast day, many believed in his name, when they saw the miracles which he did.

JOHN 3:18
18 He that believeth on him is not condemned: but he that believeth not is condemned already, because he hath not believed in the name of the only begotten Son of God.

JOHN 14:13,14
13 And whatsoever ye shall ask in my name, that will I do, that the Father may be glorified in the Son.
14 If ye shall ask any thing in my name, I will do it.

JOHN 14:26
26 But the Comforter, which is the Holy Ghost, whom the Father will send in my name, he shall teach you all things, and bring all things to your remembrance, whatsoever I have said unto you.

JOHN 15:16
16 Ye have not chosen me, but I have chosen you, and ordained you, that ye should go and bring forth fruit, and that your fruit should remain: that whatsoever ye shall ask of the Father in my name, he may give it you.

JOHN 15:20,21
20 . . . If they have persecuted me, they will also persecute you; if they have kept my saying, they will keep yours also.
21 But all these things will they do unto you for my name's sake, because they know not him that sent me.

JOHN 16:23,24,26,27

23 And in that day ye shall ask me nothing. Verily, verily, I say unto you, Whatsoever ye shall ask the Father in my name, he will give it you.

24 Hitherto have ye asked nothing in my name: ask, and ye shall receive, that your joy may be full . . . .

26 At that day ye shall ask in my name: and I say not unto you that I will pray the Father for you;

27 For the Father himself loveth you, because ye loved me, and have believed that I came from God.

JOHN 20:31

31 But these are written, that ye might believe that Jesus is the Christ, the Son of God; and that believing ye might have life through his name.

ACTS 2:21

21 And it shall come to pass, that whosoever shall call on the name of the Lord shall be saved.

ACTS 2:38

38 Then Peter said unto them, Repent, and be baptized every one of you in the name of Jesus Christ for the remission of sins, and ye shall receive the gift of the Holy Ghost.

ACTS 3:6

6 Then Peter said, Silver and gold have I none; but such as I have give I thee: In the name of Jesus Christ of Nazareth rise up and walk.

ACTS 3:16

16 And his name through faith in his name hath made this man strong, whom ye see and know: yea,

the faith which is by him hath given him this perfect soundness in the presence of you all.

ACTS 4:7,8,10,12,17,18
7 And when they had set them in the midst, they
asked, By what power, or by what name, have ye
done this?
8 Then Peter, filled with the Holy Ghost, said . . . .
10 Be it known unto you all, and to all the people
of Israel, that by the name of Jesus Christ of
Nazareth, whom ye crucified, whom God raised
from the dead, even by him doth this man stand
here before you whole . . . .
12 Neither is there salvation in any other: for there
is none other name under heaven given among
men, whereby we must be saved . . . .
17 But that it spread no further among the people,
let us straitly threaten them, that they speak henceforth to no man in this name.
18 And they called them, and commanded them not
to speak at all nor teach in the name of Jesus.

ACTS 4:29,30
29 And now, Lord, behold their threatenings: and
grant unto thy servants, that with all boldness they
may speak thy word,
30 By stretching forth thine hand to heal; and that
signs and wonders may be done by the name of thy
holy child Jesus.

ACTS 5:28
28 . . . Did not we straitly command you that ye
should not teach in this name? and, behold, ye
have filled Jerusalem with your doctrine, and
intend to bring this man's blood upon us.

ACTS 5:40-42

40 . . . and when they had called the apostles, and beaten them, they commanded that they should not speak in the name of Jesus, and let them go.

41 And they departed from the presence of the council, rejoicing that they were counted worthy to suffer shame for his name.

42 And daily in the temple, and in every house, they ceased not to teach and preach Jesus Christ.

ACTS 8:12

12 But when they believed Philip preaching the things concerning the kingdom of God, and the name of Jesus Christ, they were baptized, both men and women.

ACTS 9:14-16

14 And here he [Saul who later was named Paul] hath authority from the chief priests to bind all that call on thy name.

15 But the Lord said unto him, Go thy way: for he is a chosen vessel unto me, to bear my name before the Gentiles, and kings, and the children of Israel:

16 For I will shew him how great things he must suffer for my name's sake.

ACTS 9:21,27,29

21 But all that heard him [Paul] were amazed, and said; Is not this he that destroyed them which called on this name in Jerusalem . . . .

27 But Barnabas took him, and brought him to the apostles, and declared unto them how he had seen the Lord in the way, and that he had spoken to him, and how he had preached boldly at Damascus in the name of Jesus . . . .

29 And he spake boldly in the name of the Lord
Jesus, and disputed against the Grecians . . . .

ACTS 10:43
43 To him give all the prophets witness, that
through his name whosoever believeth in him shall
receive remission of sins.

ACTS 10:48
48 And he commanded them to be baptized in the
name of the Lord. Then prayed they him to tarry
certain days.

ACTS 15:25,26
25 It seemed good unto us, being assembled with
one accord, to send chosen men unto you with our
beloved Barnabas and Paul,
26 Men that have hazarded their lives for the name
of our Lord Jesus Christ.

ACTS 16:18
18 And this did she many days. But Paul, being
grieved, turned and said to the spirit, I command
thee in the name of Jesus Christ to come out of her.
And he came out the same hour.

ACTS 19:5
5   When they heard this, they were baptized in the
name of the Lord Jesus.

ROMANS 1:5
5   By whom we have received grace and apostle-
ship, for obedience to the faith among all nations,
for his name.

ROMANS 10:13
13 For whosoever shall call upon the name of the Lord shall be saved.

1 CORINTHIANS 1:2
2 Unto the church of God which is at Corinth, to them that are sanctified in Christ Jesus, called to be saints, with all that in every place call upon the name of Jesus Christ our Lord, both theirs and ours.

1 CORINTHIANS 1:10
10 Now I beseech you, brethren, by the name of our Lord Jesus Christ, that ye all speak the same thing, and that there be no divisions among you; but that ye be perfectly joined together in the same mind and in the same judgment.

PHILIPPIANS 2:9-11
9 Wherefore God also hath highly exalted him, and given him a name which is above every name:
10 That at the name of Jesus every knee should bow, of things in heaven, and things in earth, and things under the earth;
11 And that every tongue should confess that Jesus Christ is Lord, to the glory of God the Father.

COLOSSIANS 3:17
17 And whatsoever ye do in word or deed, do all in the name of the Lord Jesus, giving thanks to God and the Father by him.

2 THESSALONIANS 1:12
12 That the name of our Lord Jesus Christ may be glorified in you, and ye in him, according to the grace of our God and the Lord Jesus Christ.

2 TIMOTHY 2:19
19 Nevertheless the foundation of God standeth sure, having this seal, The Lord knoweth them that are his. And, Let every one that nameth the name of Christ depart from iniquity.

HEBREWS 1:4
4   Being made so much better than the angels, as he hath by inheritance obtained a more excellent name than they.

HEBREWS 6:10
10 For God is not unrighteous to forget your work and labour of love, which ye have shewed toward his name, in that ye have ministered to the saints, and do minister.

HEBREWS 13:15
15 By him therefore let us offer the sacrifice of praise to God continually, that is, the fruit of our lips giving thanks to his name.

JAMES 5:14
14 Is any sick among you? let him call for the elders of the church; and let them pray over him, anointing him with oil in the name of the Lord.

1 PETER 4:14
14 If ye be reproached for the name of Christ, happy are ye; for the spirit of glory and of God resteth upon you: on their part he is evil spoken of, but on your part he is glorified.

1 JOHN 2:12
12 I write unto you, little children, because your sins are forgiven you for his name's sake.

1 JOHN 3:23
23 And this is his commandment, That we should believe on the name of his Son Jesus Christ, and love one another, as he gave us commandment.

1 JOHN 5:13
13 These things have I written unto you that believe on the name of the Son of God; that ye may know that ye have eternal life, and that ye may believe on the name of the Son of God.

REVELATION 19:12,13,16
12 His eyes were as a flame of fire, and on his head were many crowns; and he had a name written, that no man knew, but he himself.
13 And he was clothed with a vesture dipped in blood: and his name is called The Word of God . . . .
16 And he hath on his vesture and on his thigh a name written, KING OF KINGS, AND LORD OF LORDS.

REVELATION 22:3,4
3   And there shall be no more curse: but the throne of God and of the Lamb shall be in it; and his servants shall serve him:
4   And they shall see his face; and his name shall be in their foreheads.

ABOUT THE AUTHOR

Kenneth Hagin Jr., Executive Vice-President of Kenneth Hagin Ministries and Pastor of RHEMA Bible Church, teaches from a rich and diversified background of more than thirty-five years in the ministry.

Rev. Hagin Jr. attended Southwestern Assemblies of God College and graduated from Oral Roberts University with a degree in religious education. He also holds an honorary Doctor of Divinity degree from Faith Theological Seminary in Tampa, Florida.

After serving as an associate pastor, Rev. Hagin Jr. traveled as an evangelist throughout the United States and abroad and was responsible for organizing RHEMA Bible Training Center, a school which equips men and women for the ministry.

In addition to his administrative and teaching responsibilities at RHEMA, Rev. Hagin Jr. is pastor of RHEMA Bible Church, a large, thriving congregation on the RHEMA campus. He is also International Director of RHEMA Ministerial Association International, has a weekly radio program, "RHEMA Radio Church," which is heard on stations throughout the United States, and a television program, "RHEMA Praise."

The Word of Faith

The Word of Faith is a full-color monthly magazine with faith-building teaching articles by Rev. Kenneth E. Hagin and Rev. Kenneth Hagin Jr.

The Word of Faith also includes encouraging true-life stories of Christians overcoming circumstances through God's Word, and information on the various outreaches of Kenneth Hagin Ministries and RHEMA Bible Church.

To receive a free subscription to
The Word of Faith, call:

1-888-28-FAITH — Offer #603
(1-888-283-2484)

To use our Internet address:
http://www.rhema.org

RHEMA
Bible Training Center

Providing Skilled Laborers for the End-Time Harvest!

Do you desire —

- to find and effectively fulfill God's plan for your life?
- to know how to "rightly divide the Word of truth"?
- to learn how to follow and flow with the Spirit of God?
- to run your God-given race with excellence and integrity?
- to become not only a laborer but a *skilled* laborer?

If so, then RHEMA Bible Training Center is here for you!

For a free video and full-color catalog, call:

1-888-28-FAITH — Offer #602
(1-888-283-2484)

To use our Internet address:
http://www.rhema.org

RHEMA Bible Training Center admits students of any race, color, or ethnic origin.

ANOTHER LOOK AT FAITH

Kenneth Hagin Jr. • Item #733

This book focuses on what faith is not, thus answering common misunderstandings of what it means to live by faith.

THE BELIEVER'S AUTHORITY

Kenneth E. Hagin • Item #406

This powerful book provides excellent insight into the authority that rightfully belongs to every believer in Christ!

BLESSED IS . . . Untying the 'NOTS' That Hinder Your Blessing!

Kenneth Hagin Jr. • Item #736

This book creatively teaches believers from Psalm 1 what *not* to do in order to be blessed by God and receive His richest and best!

DON'T QUIT! YOUR FAITH WILL SEE YOU THROUGH

Kenneth Hagin Jr. • Item #724

Learn how you can develop faith that won't quit and come out of tests or trials victoriously.

FAITH FOOD DEVOTION

Kenneth E. Hagin • Item # 045

Rev. Kenneth E. Hagin's beautiful, hardcover devotional book, *Faith Food Devotions*, contains 356 bite-sized teachings and faith-filled confessions for triumphant Christian living every day of the year!

FOLLOWING GOD'S PLAN FOR YOUR LIFE

Kenneth E. Hagin • Item #519

It's up to individual Christians to fulfill the divine purpose that God ordained for their lives before the beginning of time. This book can help believers stay on the course God has set before them!

Book Favorites

GOD'S WORD: A Never-Failing Remedy

Kenneth E. Hagin • Item #526

The never-failing remedy for every adversity of life can be found in the pages of God's holy written Word! And when you act on the Word, it truly becomes a never-failing remedy!

THE HEALING ANOINTING

Kenneth E. Hagin • Item #527

This dynamic book explores the operation of God's powerful anointing in divine healing.

HEALING: Forever Settled

Kenneth Hagin Jr. • Item #723

The primary question among believers is whether it's God's will to heal people today. Healing is a forever-settled subject because God's Word is forever settled!

HOW TO LIVE WORRY-FREE

Kenneth Hagin Jr. • Item #735

Sound teaching from God's Word is combined with practical insights to illustrate the perils of worry and to help guide the believer into the peace of God.

HOW YOU CAN BE LED BY THE SPIRIT OF GOD

Kenneth E. Hagin • Item #513

These step-by-step guidelines based on the Scriptures can help Christians avoid spiritual pitfalls and follow the Spirit of God in every area of life.

IT'S YOUR MOVE!

Kenneth Hagin Jr. • Item #730

Move out of the arena of discouragement and despair and into the arena of God's blessings that are yours in Christ.

BOOK FAVORITES

JESUS — NAME ABOVE ALL NAMES

Kenneth Hagin Jr. • Item #523

This exciting book discusses the redemption realities and blessings that every believer inherits at salvation through the power of Jesus' Name.

LOVE: The Way to Victory

Kenneth E. Hagin • Item #523

By acting on the truths contained in this book, believers can turn around seemingly impossible situations in their lives — just by walking in the God-kind of love!

THE TRIUMPHANT CHURCH:
Dominion Over All the Powers of Darkness

Kenneth E. Hagin • Item #520

This bestseller is a comprehensive biblical study of the origin and operation of Satan that shows believers how to enforce his defeat in their lives.

THE UNTAPPED POWER IN PRAISE

Kenneth Hagin Jr. • Item #725

The power of God is available to set believers free. This book teaches how to tap into that power through praise!

WELCOME TO GOD'S FAMILY:
A Foundational Guide for Spirit-Filled Living

Kenneth E. Hagin • Item #528

Increase your spiritual effectiveness by discovering what it means to be born again and how you can partake of the biblical benefits that God has provided for you as His child!

WHAT TO DO WHEN FAITH SEEMS WEAK AND VICTORY LOST

Kenneth E. Hagin • Item #501

The ten steps outlined in this book can bring any believer out of defeat into certain victory!